JOURNEYING TOWARDS
FAITH

— Becoming What I Am —

PHILIP CARTER

Published in Australia by
Coventry Press
33 Scoresby Road
Bayswater VIC 3153

ISBN 9781922589484

Copyright © Philip Carter 2024

All rights reserved. Other than for the purposes and subject to the conditions prescribed under the *Copyright Act*, no part of this publication may be reproduced, stored in a retrieval system, or transmitted in any form or by any means, electronic, mechanical, photocopying, recording or otherwise, without the prior permission of the publisher.

Scripture quotations are from the *New Revised Standard Version Bible*, copyright 1989, Division of Christian Education of the National Council of the Churches of Christ in the United States of America. Used by permission. All rights reserved.

Catalogue-in-Publication entry is available from the National Library of Australia
http://catalogue.nla.gov.au

Cover design by Ian James – www.jgd.com.au
Text design by Coventry Press
Set in EB Garamond

Printed in Australia

Contents

Preface	5
Acknowledgments	9

Chapter One
    'Stretching toward belief'
    Exploring our pre-religious God awareness
	13

Chapter Two Jesus is the question God asks	23
Chapter Three Jesus is the parable of God	31

Chapter Four
    'We have in us a marvellous mixture of
    well-being and woe'
	42

Chapter Five
    'Listen to the language of your wounds'
    Living in a wounded and wounding world
	51

Chapter Six
    Prayer
    'God's breath in man returning to his birth'
	59

Chapter Seven
    The Prayer of Asking
    'What we most truly want is what we most
    really are'
	70

Preface

> *'If God is God, he is likely to be the most common of human experiences: people keep bumping into him all the time, but that is not what they call him.'*
>
> John V. Taylor

These seven chapters focus on what it is to be human. By taking the Incarnation seriously, their underlying assumption is that Jesus did not come to offer us a particular way of being religious, but a universal way of being human. By paying attention to the ordinary, everyday experiences we all have, we recognise that there are moments in our lives which carry with them a 'pressure of significance'. These moments open up for us encounters with the Beyond in our midst, and assure us that 'there is another world, but it is in this one'. Here and now is the right place for us, the place where we can discover our capacity for the infinite.

> *'I saw that I could not truly say "I believe" unless it was another way of saying "I am"'*
>
> H. A. Williams

Of course, this way of being in the world has its difficulties, caught as we so often are in the illusions and prejudices that plague our minds. We get side-tracked in our vulnerability into thinking that faith is simply a matter of certainty and doctrinal assent. But the seeds of faith begin to grow when we realise that the questions Jesus so often asks are not about wanting answers from us: he is wanting us, he is wanting our hearts. Which suggests that learning to live and love the questions – Jesus' questions and our questions – means that we are being asked to have our thinking about God and ourselves utterly transformed.

> *'Jesus not only utters the message of the Kingdom of God: he himself is the message.'*
>
> C. Maurer

'Waking up' is a good phrase to capture what it is that Jesus is asking of us: waking up to the fact that he is the truth of our existence, and that his dying is our dying, his life is our life, and his story is our story. As God's parable, he is simply asking us to live our lives openly and freely, in the knowledge that our experience of God will always be a lived experience from within ourselves: where we discover that 'there are answers we are the solution to'. However important our minds and reasoning are, it is the secret and hidden place of our hearts where God speaks directly to us. As Pascal saw: 'The heart has its reasons which reason doesn't know about'.

> *'... behind and beneath the smooth wheels of the socially constructed world are two abiding facts: unreconciled pain and unexhausted compassion, the history of men and women and the history of God with them (with us).'*
>
> Rowan Williams

As we struggle with our questions and doubts, and as we so often wish that our global, social and personal worlds were different, we begin, in our 'stretching toward belief' that this place we find ourselves in – full of contradiction and inconsistencies – is in fact our place, and the right place for us. For it is here, wrestling with this 'marvellous mixture of well-being and woe' that characterises all our lives, where we begin to realise how we are so easily dominated by regrets about the past and worries about the future. In facing this truth about ourselves, and living in the present moment – quietening our minds and opening our hearts – we can embrace this fundamental paradox, and awaken to the opportunity to move towards both freedom and life.

Preface

> *'I shall try to keep the wound from healing, in recognition of our living still in the old order of things. I shall try to keep it from healing, in solidarity with those who sit beside me on humanity's mourning bench.'*
>
> Nicholas Wolterstorff

The stark reality of living in the present moment, with our eyes and ears wide open, is that we realise that we live in a wounded and wounding world, that we are victims and the maker of victims. By learning to listen to the language of our wounds, we hear God's invitation to see in Jesus our 'forgiving victim'. Here new life opens up for us with new possibilities. The astounding truth of Jesus – which he lived out to the full – is that this place of wounding, this place of poverty, is the right place for us, and that it is here, where the seeds of faith, love and hope can germinate and grow.

> *'Prayer and love are learned in the hour when prayer becomes impossible and your heart has turned to stone.'*
>
> Thomas Merton

Here then is where we learn to pray, or better still, where we learn to let God pray in us. And the starting point for this to happen will always be the crisis of faith, where we realise that we cannot pray. George Herbert said that prayer is 'God's breath in man returning to his birth'. And Thomas Merton could exclaim: 'What I do is live. How I pray, is breathe'. The Genesis story tells of how the first human being was made out of the dust of the earth, and God breathed into him and made him a living being. By focusing on our breathing, we realise that we are utterly dependent creatures, but, in our interconnected-ness with the dust of the earth, with all of creation, with all of humanity, and with the community of Love which is the Trinity, we begin to experience a primordial 'yes' that is not our own, but the mysterious 'Yes' of Being itself.

> *'But it is he who prays within us and answers the prayer which is his gift.'*
>
> Petru Dumitriu

It is with this sense of inter-connectedness with everything that is, with the cosmos, with each other in the human community, and with God, that we discover the key to life. We have seen it so visibly expressed in Jesus of Nazareth, for in him we see that we are both Christologically and Paschally structured, with an in-built capacity for self-transcendence. We flourish when we give ourselves away, and find ourselves falling in love with love. In experiencing this gift we realise that God is intimately and immediately, deeply and profoundly present to the whole of creation, and our prayer – especially our intercessory prayer – becomes, not a request, but an awareness, expression and celebration of this fundamental truth.

John V. Taylor, quoted in Michael Paul Gallagher, *Free to Believe: Ten Steps to Faith*, DLT, London, 1996, 97.

H. A. Williams, *Some Day I'll Find You*, Collins Fount Paperbacks, London, 1984, 213.

C. Maurer, quoted in Joachim Jeremias, *Rediscovering the Parables*, SCM Press Ltd, London 1963, 180.

Rowan Williams, 'Sermon for Palm Sunday', *Open to Judgement: Sermons and Addresses*, DLT, London, 1994, 55.

Nicholas Wolterstorff, *Lament for a Son*, Eerdmans, Grand Rapids, 1987, 61.

Thomas Merton, *New Seeds of Contemplation*, A New Directions Book, New York, 1972, 221.

Petru Dumitriu, *Incognito*. transl. by Norman Denny, Collins, London, 1964, 358.

Acknowledgments

All that I have written has been written on the traditional land of Australia's First peoples – the Kaurna people. I pay my respects to the traditional people of this land, past, present and to come. I express gratitude in the sharing of this land, sorrow for the personal, spiritual and cultural costs of that sharing, and my hope that we may walk together in harmony, in the spirit of Reconciliation.

After fifteen years in parish ministry, I was appointed by the then Archbishop of Adelaide, Keith Rayner, to a Ministry in Spirituality based at the Diocesan Retreat House in Belair in 1988. Then, in 1997, I opened an independent, ecumenical spiritual centre called the Julian Centre at Mile End, close to the CBD of Adelaide. I ran that centre until the end of 2009 when I retired.

In 1988, I began sending out a quarterly newsletter called *Directions*, which gave information about the four Directed Retreats I ran each year, as well as regular Quiet Days of Reflection, Workshops on Prayer and Meditation, and Formation Courses in Spiritual Direction. But the other principal purpose of *Directions* was to offer, every three months, quotations, reflections and questions to do with a particular aspect of the spiritual life. Over those twenty-two years, I gathered together a large amount of material to do with the spiritual life: issues focused on Benedict, Julian, Francis and Ignatius, and some of the major themes in the tradition, including Trinitarian Spirituality, Theological Reflection, The Bread of Life, Discernment, and Faith, Love and Hope.

A few years after I retired, I realised that I could use much of this material in the writing of articles. I sent my first article to *Presence*, the journal of Spiritual Directors International based in the United States, and then an article to *Eremos*, a journal exploring spirituality in Australia. While *Presence* dealt mainly with articles on the art and practice of spiritual direction, *Eremos* published articles about personal experience and the spiritual journey, and how these affect our work in the world. This book includes four articles previously published in *Eremos*, to which I have added three further unpublished articles. I am very grateful to the two Editors of *Eremos*, Frances MacKay and John Foulcher, that I have dealt with over the past few years, for their editorial help and encouragement.

Joseph Campbell, in *The Power of Myth*, wrote:

> 'People say that what we're all seeking is a meaning for life. I don't think that's what we're really seeking. I think that what we're seeking is an experience of being alive, so that our life's experiences on the purely physical plane will have resonances within our innermost being and reality, so that we actually feel the rapture of being alive.'

Similarly, John V. Taylor, wrote in *A Matter of Life and Death*:

> 'It has long been my conviction that God is not hugely concerned as to whether we are religious or not. What matters to God, and matters supremely, is whether we are alive or not. If your religion brings you more fully to life, God will be in it: but if your religion inhibits your capacity for life or makes you run away from it, you may be sure God is against it, just as Jesus was.'

And the American farmer, ecologist and poet Wendell Berry wrote:

> 'The question before me, now that I
> am old, is not how to be dead,
> which I know from enough practice,
> but how to be alive...'

I have only quoted three writers, but I am immensely grateful to the countless writers from their different communities of faith who have spoken their truth only to resonate with mine. The Incarnation – which says so much about God and at the same time so much about the mystery of being human – is a central

Acknowledgments

impetus for me towards life and freedom, and the joy of becoming what I am, and hearing an invitation to be both fully alive and fully human. This, as I see it, is the great journey of faith. As Ireneaus, in the first century, saw so clearly: 'The glory of God is a human being fully alive'. This does not lead us to gloss over or deny the difficulties and challenges being human present, but rather encourages us to further commit ourselves to all our fellow human beings, as well as working towards an ecologically healthier environment and a safer and more just world. Life asks of us an unabashed passion for the truth. It does not ask us to evade or fudge the bewilderment, the ambiguity and the not-knowing which is so much a part of all our lives. But if all this demands of us a stance of 'wholly attending', it also asks us to remember, as G. K. Chesterton wrote, the 'forgotten blaze or burst of astonishment at our own existence'.

Over the years, I have received enormous encouragement from colleagues and friends in the work that I did in and through the Julian Centre. I am very grateful to the many people who have supported the Julian Centre and to those who have contributed financially to this ministry, and particularly to Valerie Taylor, whose generosity allowed us to form The Julian Centre Trust. I am particularly grateful to Jonathan Wells who has been a friend and great supporter of my ministry: to Maxine Smith, who was Administrative Assistant at the Julian Centre: and to Faye Lindsay, who helped with reception at the Centre on Fridays. A particular gift for me has been the opportunity to travel to Malaysia over ten times in the past twenty years to offer Directed and Preached Retreats, where I have been given hospitality and encouragement, and made many friends.

I need to mention also the precious gift that the spiritual direction community, here and overseas, has been to me. I am particularly grateful to Helen, who has quietly supported me in the various ministries I have been involved in over the years

Philip Carter
August 2023

Chapter One

'Stretching toward belief'[1]

Exploring our pre-religious God awareness[2]

'There is another world, but it is in this one.'[3]

'The sacred must be rediscovered in what moves and touches us, in what makes us tremble, in what is proximate rather than remote, ordinary rather than extraordinary, native rather than imported.'[4] What Sam Keen suggests here is that every experience we have, every event and every person we meet, offers us the potential of being an epiphany of the divine presence. For this potential to be realised, we need to recover 'a sense of "beyondness" in the midst of the whole of life to revive the springs of wonder and adoration'.[5] But as the Russian writer, Solzhenitsyn, commented in 1983: 'The great crisis of humanity today is that it has lost its sense of the invisible'.[6]

---

1 Luci Shaw, '... for they shall see God', *Polishing the Petoskey Stone, New & Selected Poems*, Harold Shaw, Illinois, 1990, 154.
2 First published in *Eremos* August 2023. Reprinted by permission.
3 Paul Eluard, quoted on the title page of Patrick White, *The Solid Mandala*, Penguin, 1969.
4 Sam Keen, *To a Dancing God*, Harper & Row, New York, 1970.
5 John V. Taylor, *The Go-Between God: The Holy Spirit and the Christian Mission*, SCM, London, 1972, 45.
6 Solzhenitsyn, quoted in Michael Whelan SM, *Without God All things Are Lawful*, St Pauls, Sydney, 1995, 2.

We live in a sacramental universe: everything that meets our gaze, that touches us or moves us, 'is a parable veiling and unveiling its higher meaning',[7] a visible or tangible sign of an invisible grace or gift. Jesus, as the parable of God, makes clear that the locus of revelation is the living and lived experience of humanity. As the Second Vatican Council document *Gaudium et Spes* says, it is Jesus who 'worked with human hands, thought with a human mind, acted by human choice, and loved with a human heart'.[8]

Just as Jesus knew he was loved, sent, known and one with the One he called Father, so he opens up for us his lived human experience as the template for our own experience of the Divine. As the parable of God, Jesus is not taking us out of this world, but inviting us to become aware of the invisible transcendence that not only touches our ordinary reality but disrupts it. The parable, just like Jesus, doesn't so much teach us as 'invites and surprises [us] into an experience' that can be both revelatory and transformative.[9]

There are many and varied phrases to name this experience of the 'Other', as we wrestle with the givenness of our reality, and to come to terms with 'what we happen to apprehend directly with our five senses' is not all the reality there is. Philip Toynbee became convinced that 'there must be more than this'. This realisation became for him 'the bedrock of whatever religious faith I have'.[10] Of course, however hard we try to comprehend these moments of recognition that 'there must be more than this', we will never succeed, and yet, 'through striving to see it, through longing for it ... [we] will succeed in preserving it as an eternal possibility'.[11]

---

7 Hugo Rahner, quoted in Eugene Stockton, *Wonder: A Way to God*, St Pauls, 1998, 29.
8 *The Documents of Vatican II*, ed. Walter M. Abbot, S.J., Geoffrey Chapman, London, 1966, Section 22.
9 Sally McFague, *Speaking in Parables*, SCM, London, 1975, 65.
10 Philip Toynbee, *End of a Journey: An Autobiographical Journal 1979-1981*, Bloomsbury, 1988, 9.
11 R. S. Thomas, *Selected Prose*, ed. Sandra Anstey, Poetry Wales Press, Mid Glamorgan, 1983, 164.

These moments we apprehend, rather than comprehend, are 'moments of grace', 'events of the Spirit', 'rumours of angels', 'signals of transcendence'. Les Murray, the Australian poet, speaks of a 'world ... resonant and radiant with meanings', events and moments in our lives where we experience, in his pregnant and wonderful phrase, a 'pressure of significance'.[12] 'To sense', as Albert Einstein declared, 'that behind everything that can be experienced there is something that our minds cannot grasp, whose beauty and sublimity reaches us only indirectly: this is religiousness. In this sense, and in this sense only, I am a devoutly religious man.'[13]

Our relationship with the Divine is not some kind of indoctrination from outside us but something which awakens us from within, an 'inescapable situation of all being to be involved in the infinite mystery. We may continue to disregard the mystery but we can neither deny nor escape it'.[14] The critique Jesus makes again and again of the human condition is that our eyes are closed and we cannot see clearly, that we are too often hard-hearted, and that our minds cannot bear too much reality.

The beatitude of Jesus, that we are blessed, that we are in the right place when we are poor in spirit, points to an inner revolution in the way we see ourselves, our world and God, turning us upside down and inside out, inviting us into a truth that grasps us, rather than a truth that we can grasp, and into a vison that demands both humility and vulnerability. 'At the core of [our] existence a "transcendental neediness" holds sway [which] spurs and supports all our longings and desires.'[15] Jesus' own poverty of Spirit, his experience of vulnerability, is the very truth of our existence as

---

12 Les Murray, quoted in David Tacey, *Re-Enchantment: The New Australian Spirituality*, HarperCollins, Sydney, 2000, 112.
13 Albert Einstein, *On Cosmic Religion and Other Opinions and Aphorisms*, Dover Publications, NY, 2009.
14 Rabbi Abraham Joshua Heschel, *God in Search of Man*, Straus & Giroux, NY, 1976.
15 Johannes B. Metz, *Poverty of Spirit*, Newman Press, NY, 1968, 28.

human beings, calling us to live our truth in such a way that leads to life. He was always concerned to shape our attitude, the disposition of our hearts: he wanted to lead us to those hidden depths in us where our God-given life is attempting to grow. However

> *For most of us, there is only the unattended*
> *Moment, the moment in and out of time,*
> *The distraction fit, lost in a shaft of sunlight.*[16]

God reveals God's self, albeit in many ways hidden and obscured, and wants us to wake up, and see a little more clearly, and recover the 'vision splendid' of the Divine in the midst of our lives. This is our life's task, 'breaking out of the prison-house of the ego into a second childhood, into childhood transfigured'.[17] We are diggers, not builders, in a world where God comes to us disguised as our life, and learning Jesus, rather than claiming even to know him is our task: patiently learning his very true and human way of living in this world, respectfully listening and gently touching the Divine engagement with the world. If it is true, that for most of us, most of the time, 'there is only the unattended moment', the first inkling of 'there must be more than this' could be seen as a kind of religious conversion, what I am calling a pre-religious experience, and one which is prior to any explicit Christian interpretation.

Such experiences are not starting a person's relationship with the Divine but simply advancing it, and invite us to live in this world by attention. I have, with many others, an ever-growing conviction that in this post-modern world, the real crisis facing the churches is not dwindling numbers, nor the need for more relevance in worship and preaching, nor more missionary zeal to counteract the slow death of Christian faith. 'The widespread ineffectiveness of organised religion today is due to the failure to speak to [our] pre-religious God awareness.'[18]

---

16 T. S. Eliot, 'The Dry Salvages', *Four Quartets*, Faber and Faber, London, 1959, 44.
17 Donald Nicholl, *Holiness*, DLT, London 1981, 149.
18 Sebastian Moore, *The Fire and the Rose are One*, DLT, London, 1980, 35.

Discovering our capacity for the infinite

In his Christmas homily at the beginning of the new Millennium, John Paul II referred to the immortal genius of Michelangelo in his painting on the ceiling of the Sistine Chapel, 'the moment when God the Father communicated the gift of life to the first man [Adam] and made him "a living being". Between the finger of God and the finger of man stretching out to each other and almost touching, there seems to be an invisible spark: God communicates to man a tremor of his own life, creating him in his image and likeness. The divine breath is the origin of the unique dignity of every human being, of humanity's boundless yearning for the infinite'.[19]

So many of us, in our search for significance or meaning, wrestle constantly with our understanding of God, and fail to detect the clue to our search that lies in the human heart. 'God is not exterior evidence, but the secret call within us',[20] or as the poet-priest R. S. Thomas puts it: *'There are questions we are the solution/to'*.[21] The human heart carries within it a memory of something that is ours but what has been lost. Ronald Rolheiser talks of how each of us has been kissed before we were born, kissed and caressed by God so that we carry with us all our life that precious, and dark, memory. I live my life with this memory forever etched in my heart: I am, because of this kiss, always looking for something that I have already, appreciating beauty or truth because they resonate with something deep within me. And when I am hurt or abused, I experience a dissonance within that does not match that perfect caress.[22]

Our hearts are indeed restless: we want more, we yearn for transcendence, wisdom and hope; we sense our own darkness, and

---

19 John Paul II, quoted in Daniel O'Leary, *Begin with the Heart: Recovering a Sacramental Vision*, The Columba Press, Dublin, 2008, 152.
20 Olivier Clement, quoted in Kallistos Ware, *The Orthodox Way*, St. Vladimir's Seminary Press, NY, 2002.
21 R. S. Thomas, 'Emerging', *Collected Poems*, J.M. Dent, London, 1993, 263.
22 Ronald Rolheiser, http://ronrolheiser, 'Dark Memory', 16 October 1997.

we ache for the reassurance of a larger story than our own, that includes us, and satisfies our longing to make sense of our existence.

The truth about ourselves (a truth our indigenous sisters and brothers know) is that we are spiritual beings struggling to be truly human. Most of us, I suspect, are human beings struggling to be spiritual. What we have already seen is that, if God is God, then we will be meeting God in everything that we experience, though we might not name that encounter as a God-encounter. We do not project or create God into our lived experience, but find God already there, present to us and within us, and inviting us to open our eyes and our minds and our hearts to the divine reality.

Experiencing ourselves is the key and the condition for experiencing God. A Christian anthropology, understanding what it means to be human in the light of God's revelation in Jesus, is vital: Jesus is the very truth of our existence, his inner experience of openness, trust and love that he shared with his God, whom he called Father, speaks directly into our own experience of openness and capacity for God as well.

Just as Jesus in his inner experience, in his vulnerability and poverty lived selflessly for others, and indeed for the Other, so our starting point for our search to become more fully human, will be in growing into those things that 'take us outside of ourselves', and so reflect in our way of life our very human capacity to transcend ourselves. The great gift Jesus brings us is surely our discovery that, made as we are in the image of God, our hearts are already open to God. Because God is immediately and intimately present to us all the time, it is not just those incidents and circumstances outside ourselves that attract us (moments when we are confronted by the beauty or tragedy of nature, when we are immersed in the little things that stop us in our tracks, or when the sky's expanse or the vastness of the ocean speaks to us) that can become starting points for faith.

There are also the very human, personal experiences of life and of being human that all of us carry: our experiences of relationships, offering us the possibilities of intimacy, love and self-forgetfulness, but also the often inevitable hurts that relationships bring – owning up to our own wounds and woundedness which offer the possibility of living with our egos differently; pain as we look around our social and larger world, and the feelings of impotence and hopelessness that brings, as well the invitation to find the courage to take even a very small step to make a difference: our attempts at overcoming loneliness and finding inner strength and a sense of worth through solitude; and living in the crucible of the ordinary with both its limitations and its possibilities.[23]

As well as this way of seeing the potential hidden in the 'limit experiences' of our lives, we can also get in touch with what Peter Berger calls 'signals of transcendence'. He talks of our instinct towards order, and our fundamental, though sorely tested trust in reality: those moments where we suspend the stark realities of time and death and touch the impetus and gift of eternity embedded in our instinct towards play; our brush with evil, in its many forms, and our need to condemn it; our sense of humour, recognising the paradoxes of life with its inevitable mixture of joy and tragedy, and our basic instinct to push against the finiteness of the human condition, to keep on hoping when all hope seems lost.[24]

Becoming what I am

The starting points for faith, the things that help us 'grope' and 'stretch' for a way of life that will lead to life, are everywhere around and within us. Already immersed in mystery, we are met by a presence that is simply a gracious availability; a presence that we apprehend but cannot comprehend. This mystery is not *how* the world is, but *that* the world is. It is a mystery that is always enough and never enough. It is a mystery of a God who is co-present in every human experience, evoking in us 'hints followed by guesses'; a mystery both known and unknown, where

---

23 Michael Paul Gallagher, *Dive Deeper: The Human Poetry of Faith*, DLT, London, 2001, 94-95.
24 Peter L. Berger, *A Rumour of Angels: Modern Society and the Rediscovery of the Supernatural*, Penguin Books, Harmondsworth, 1971, 169.

'we find ourselves *addressed*, and addressed, we *find* ourselves'.[25] This mystery calls from us a response that is completely at one with the deepest yearnings of our hearts. It is the longing for depth and meaning, purpose and silence, solitude and creativity, wisdom and joy, healing and transcendence, and deep connection and communion with all that is.

This mystery, the 'context and horizon' of our lives, is our deepest truth, though we are so often unaware of its richness and treasure. We only make sense of our lives when we are in touch with what is beyond us. Such is the mystery that calls out from us not a proof of God's existence, but a lived, deeply felt appreciation that all we can offer is our poverty and emptiness, the very shape of the human heart. This mystery cannot be defined or fully understood. Like a parable, it stops short of explaining itself: it is evocative, and releases in us a power that is beyond us.

The primordial reality of the human heart is a mysterious and hidden place where we either journey towards 'authentic self-discovery' through self-giving, or refuse to do so. This power is born out of the humble beginnings of recognising the 'signals of transcendence' and the 'pressure of significance'. It is a power that then begins to meet our deep need for recognition and to accept that in some sense we matter, so we can simply affirm 'I am' and live in such a way that we can be true to ourselves and discover the freedom that brings.

It is now I can begin to face how readily I fall into living with a mistaken identity.[26] The person I normally think I am – the 'little' self, pre-occupied with busyness and anxieties, goals and issues – is only remotely a very small part of who I really am. Too often I tend to seek fulfilment at this level, which means I miss out on what life can really offer me. No wonder Jesus said that the one who tries to 'keep' her life (her 'little' life) loses it, but the one who is willing to

---

25 Sarah Bachelard, *Experiencing God in a Time of Crisis*, Convivium Press, Miami, Florida, 2012, 36.
26 Cynthia Bourgeault, *Centering Prayer and Inner Awakening*, Cowley, Plymouth, 2004, 10.

lose it will find the life that is life indeed (Matthew 16:25). Hidden beneath the 'noise' of the smaller 'I' with all its demands is a deeper and more authentic self – the treasure all of us live with every day. Unfortunately, we too often fail either to notice it or live into its invitation.

To be able to say 'I am' is God's great gift to us. Whether it is in the whole of the created order and this sacramental world, or in the intimacy of our personal lives, to hear a 'pressure of significance' whispering to us and inviting us and 'taking us outside of ourselves', is the discovery of what it really means to be an authentic human being. The 'other' – however the 'other' manifests itself to us, through seeing and hearing, touching and tasting what this natural world has to offer or through the persons that inhabit our daily lives – is none other than the ultimate 'Other', who is constantly and committedly calling us to be fully ourselves, so that we discover the 'unique dignity' of the human being.

It is as if we have a God-shaped hole in our hearts that yearns to be filled, an inner core of a Spirit-led desire for more, well before we ever arrive at any explicitly Christian interpretations of our existence. Long before we make any claim for anything explicitly religious, 'we have to do something about the fire that burns within us. What we do with that fire, [and] how we channel it, the disciplines and habits we choose to live by, will either lead to greater integration or disintegration within our bodies, minds and souls'.[27] The new life that we are beginning to wake up to, through the dispositions we bring to our everyday and very real experience, is not a possession, not worked out as a result of our reasoning powers so much as the openness of our hearts towards the ever-expanding horizon of the mystery that we are a part of. The words of Jesus speak directly into our condition: 'If only you knew the gift of God, and who it is that is speaking to you' (John 3:10).

---

[27] Ronald Rolheiser, *Seeking Spirituality: Guidelines for a Christian Spirituality for the Twenty-First Century*, Hodder & Stoughton, 1998, 11.

Learning to live in this way means that we are beginning to see faith not as a noun but as a verb, a process, an encounter that helps us to transcend the unreality with which we too often surround ourselves. Faith asks not to fit ourselves into a set of truths or propositions, but rather to be liberated from being too closely allied to religious belief or even religious belonging which can inhibit the impetus towards truth and life that springs from within us. If we can be less strident and even less certain – attitudes which can often hide our fear or anxiety – and become more aware and in touch with our depths and our hungers, we will become more open to the possibility of a real and living faith.

One of the things our minds do is to set up belief and unbelief, faith and doubt, in opposition, whereas our hearts know better. This is precisely what Jesus touched, spoke to, and aroused in those he met. What is called for is a fundamental openness of heart, and the readiness to see and hear what is really there, and the refusal 'to tamper with reality, no matter how frightening or costly it appears to be...' so that we can be 'interiorly taught by God'.[28] Or, in Michael Leunig's words: 'We shall rescue the entombed heart. We shall bring it to the surface, to the light and air. We shall nurse it and listen respectfully to its story'.[29]

Faith is certainly no acquired accomplishment. It is an ongoing process, coming to us as gift: we are stretching toward belief. It is certainly a way of being in the world, with all its paradoxes and ambiguities, and has the potential of tapping into the hidden and rich place of the human heart, to offer us the possibility of life and freedom, courage and hope. The world of which we are a part, and our own interior hearts, minds and imaginations, offer us, in T. S. Eliot's words, 'hints and guesses' – indeed

> *Hints followed by guesses; and the rest*
> *Is prayer, observance, discipline, thought and action.*
> *The hint half guessed, the gift half understood, is Incarnation.*[30]

---

28 Sandra Schneiders, *Written That You may Believe: Encountering Jesus in the Fourth Gospel*, Herder & Herder, NY, 1999, 88.
29 Michael Leunig, *A Common Prayer*, Dove Publications, Victoria, 1990.
30 T. S. Eliot, op. cit.

Chapter Two

Jesus is the question God asks[31]

There's a famous bit of graffiti written on a railway station wall: 'Jesus is the answer'. Someone has written below it: 'But what was the question?' The heart of meaning for the Christian lies in the story of Jesus of Nazareth, and his story's intersection with the human story. For Jesus is the self-expression and self-communication of God, and he meets us in our experiences of vulnerability, pain, loss and joy. And because of that intersection, faith will always involve questioning and struggle. For the truth Jesus offers is a startling and radical re-ordering and re- orientation of what we can say about God and the human person.

Jesus challenges our long-held assumptions and illusions about God, our very religiosity. As Rowan Williams suggests in *The Wound of Knowledge*: 'the questioning involved here is not our interrogation of the data, but its interrogation of us.'[32] He continues: 'the greatness of the great Christian saints lies in their readiness to be questioned, judged, stripped naked and left speechless by that which lies at the centre of their faith'. The truth of Jesus which strikes so radically and poignantly at the human condition is that the self-emptying of God in the Incarnation, where we see God in Jesus utterly vulnerable and defenceless in the face of a hostile and violent world, is mirrored in a very human Jesus, self-emptying and defenceless in the face of the same hostile and violent world. Our questions remain: just who is this Jesus of Nazareth? But embedded in our relentless questioning

---

31 First published in *Eremos* April 2022. Reprinted by permission
32 Rowan Williams, *The Wound of Knowledge*, DLT, London, 1979, 1.

is the awe-full realisation that we ourselves are the ones being interrogated.

UN Secretary General Dag Hammarskjold, who died in a plane crash in 1961, and whose personal and deeply spiritual writings were published after his death, wrote: 'I don't know Who – or-what put the question, I don't know when it was put. I don't even remember answering. But at some moment I did answer Yes to Someone – or Something – and from that hour I was certain that existence is meaningful and that, therefore, my life in self-surrender, had a purpose'.[33]

Thomas Merton characteristically exclaimed: 'God, my God, with You it is always the same thing! Always the same question that nobody knows how to answer! While I am asking questions that You do not answer, You ask me a question that is so simple that I cannot answer it. I do not even understand the question'.[34] How long will it take us to realise that the right question will constantly refresh our awareness that life is not a problem but a mystery, that the right question is there to arrest the ego's attempt to control reality?

Famously, the German poet Rainer Maria Rilke wrote in *Letters to a Young Poet*: '...be patient towards all that is unresolved in your heart and to try and love *the questions themselves* ... Do not now strive to uncover answers: they cannot be given you because you have not been able to live them. And what matters is to live everything. *Live* the questions Now. Perhaps then you will gradually, without noticing it, live your way into the answer, one distant day in the future'.[35]

In the gospels, Jesus asks questions, over three hundred of them! He is the great Interrogator. Yet he does not expect an answer so much as an answering person. His questions, like his parables,

---

33 Dag Hammarskjold, *Markings*, Faber & Faber, London, 1964, 169.
34 Thomas Merton, *The Sign of Jonas*, Harcourt Bruce & Company, Florida, 1953, 198, 353.
35 Rainer Maria Rilke, *Letters to a Young Poet*, Penguin Books, Random House, UK, 2016, 17.

seek to break open his hearers' hearts and narrow minds to the meaning of life and the mystery of God. His questions have the capacity to reposition us: they encourage us to face our illusions, challenge our images of God, ourselves and the world, and present us with an altogether new way of seeing things. His questions engage, invite and summon us: they do not condemn or put us down. They welcome us to the truth, to our truth.

Just as his life is a response to the question and call of God, Jesus wants us to make this same response. Jesus, when he asks questions, speaks out of his personal inner experience, his self-knowledge. He knows how deep our need is for answers, conclusions and control: but he wants us to find the courage to ask our own questions, and to stay on the search, to remain 'unknowing', and in the dark even, but alive and questing, reaching out to a beyond and a future that is in reality always calling us forth.

His questions reveal his compassion and love for his fellow humans. There is a lot going on when Jesus asks questions. Before he even puts the question to them, he sees them. And having asked his question, he *hears* them. And they are taken seriously, and *believed* in. While the questions often remain unanswered, it is the shock, the challenge, the invitation or the probing that remain: his questions always point beyond the obvious to that which lies hidden, even unresolved, in the human heart.

We are marked as human beings, not by our autonomy but by our receptivity and availability. We are incomplete, unfinished, but this is part of our inherent dignity and freedom. It is as if we bear a mystery in our very being, one that is often untapped, greater than ourselves. Rather than human beings we are human becomings. 'Do you love me'? (John 21:15-17) he asks. 'Do you realise what I have done for you?' (John 13:12) 'Do you believe I can do this?' (Matthew 9:28) 'Do you want to be well?' (John 5:6) 'What do you want me to do for you?' (Mark 10:36).

Elie Wiesel, the Holocaust survivor, has spoken about the word 'question': In the word *question*, there is a beautiful word – *quest*. We are all partners in a quest. The essential questions have no answers. You are my question, and I am yours – then there is dialogue. The moment we have answers, there is no dialogue. Questions unite people, answers divide them'.[36]

The Scriptures attest to the fact that human beings are addressed, created as hearers of the Word, and only in responding to the Word do we rise to our full dignity. We have been 'conceived in the mind of God as the partner in a dialogue'.[37] And this is a dialogue, between us, and between us and God, and it is not merely a communication of ideas or concepts, but communion. We are relational beings, and when the question hits that 'quest' within us, the 'the more there is that happens'. As we saw in the previous chapter, it is when we find ourselves addressed that we find ourselves.[38]

When Jesus asks that famous question, 'Who do you say I am?', he asks it in a very dramatic setting, in Caesarea Philippi. Here is a poor and homeless man from Galilee, who has gathered around him twelve ordinary men, while Jewish leaders are plotting and planning on destroying him as a dangerous heretic. The place where Jesus asks this question had long been dedicated to Syrian Gods, and to the God Pan. Here, the Temple built in honour of Caesar-God dominated the landscape. It is as if Jesus is being deliberately provocative in his question: it is a question which goes to the very heart of people's allegiances.

This question, like most of Jesus' questions, suggests that Jesus is the question that God asks, the question that God ask all of us all the time. The power of Mark's Gospel, where the question arises, lies not in what it *tells* the disciples and its readers, but in what it *asks* of them. The Jesus of Mark's Gospel provides very few answers: but the questioner himself, by asking this question, compels us to declare ourselves, and to reveal where we stand. We get a sense from this question that it has welled up from the silence deep within his experience of life and God. This is someone who knows where he comes from and where he is going. It is a question

---

36 Elie Wiesel, https://www.oprah.com/omagazine/oprah-interviews- elie wiesel/all
37 Hans Urs von Balthasar, *Prayer*, SPCK, London, 1961, 18-19.
38 Bachelard, op. cit., 36.

– as we continue to reflect on it – that is not waiting to be solved, but entered into and embrace, so that we too can enter into that ever-deepening and ever-enriching journey of self-knowledge.

When Jesus asks, 'Who do you say I am?', he is literally saying to his disciples: 'You and me both'. Jesus is moving from action to passion, and is to be at the disposal of others: and he is preparing his disciples to do the same. And that is what is so difficult to grasp and accept. God is nothing like what they – and we – had imagined. What is asked of us is precisely the same vulnerability and defencelessness that Jesus showed. As the great Protestant theologian Jurgen Moltmann puts it in *The Crucified God*: 'God is not greater than he is in this humiliation ... is not more glorious than he is in this self-surrender'.[39] This is a very radical, challenging and demanding mystery, one that is self-implicating, and hence as hard for us as it was for the disciples to fathom.

Following Jesus, as the disciples found, is not easy. There is much to digest, understand and accept. And the way we approach the questions of Jesus is vital. For disposition is everything. The stories of Jesus offer us a way of being and attending to our everyday experience, and in doing so, wake up to a hidden truth. Hesitation and attention (as Simone Weil knew) are in fact the very dispositions necessary for us to make the right response.

In Marks' Gospel, when Jesus asks, 'Who do you say I am?', it is Peter, not uncharacteristically, who jumps in with a response. And it is not long before Jesus rebukes him. Peter gets the question right, but wrong! He fails to hesitate and realise the full implication of the question, and perhaps that is a timely warning to us to spend more time listening to the question, hesitating before it, resisting a false answer, and waiting for a moment of disclosure. The question is offering us space and freedom from illusion, ingrained attitudes and prejudices.

However much we might claim to want to know the truth, we so often fail to see that we ourselves are part of the answer. It

---

39 Jurgen Moltmann, *The Crucified God*, SCM, London, 1974, 205.

is as if we can only validly say who Jesus is when we can say who we are. For the question Jesus always asks us is: 'Are you true? Are you truly present?" St Augustine famously asked: 'But where was I when I looked for you? You were there before my eyes, but I had deserted even my own self. I could not find myself, much less find you'.[40] The poet R. S. Thomas puts it succinctly: 'There are questions we are the solution/to'.[41] As Harry Williams, a member of the Community of the Resurrection, said: 'I could not truly say "I believe" unless it was another way of saying "I am"'.[42] And, of course, as many have seen, that ancient question 'Who am I?' leads inevitably to the equally important question 'Whose am I?' It is as if the questions God asks of us are always to do with our identity, integrity and authenticity.

According to Mark's Gospel, which ends abruptly with no resurrection appearances, the resurrection is not an answer but a question, the final question, reaching right into our very lives and asking of us a response. The conclusion we can draw from this is that, according to Mark, there is only one genuine way to witness the resurrection: to follow in discipleship. In Bonhoeffer's phrase: 'we shall never know what we do not do'.[43]

When Jesus asks this question, he's wanting us to grow in our understanding of God, to move from an object-subject relationship with God, to a quite radical encounter with the God who is the true subject of our being. True knowledge of God is always going to be participatory, relational and therefore something experienced from the inside out. And all our experiences of God are indirect: mediated through our everyday experience of ourselves, each other and life.

---

40 St Augustine, *Confessions*, Book V, Chapter 2, trans. R.S. Pine-Coffin, Penguin, London, 1962.
41 R. S. Thomas, 'Emerging', in *Collected Poems*, J. M. Dent, London, 1993, 263.
42 H. A. Williams, *Some Day I'll Find You*, Collins Fount Paperbacks, London, 1984, 213.
43 Bonhoeffer, quoted in John V. Taylor, *The Go-Between God*, SCM Press, London, 1972, 121.

We might say that God is co-present in everything that happens, and in our everyday experience we begin to experience God as the very basis for our seeing and knowing and valuing. As the American novelist Jane Hamilton puts it: 'For me God was something within that allowed me, occasionally, to see'.[44]

One of our problems is that we have identified objectivity with tangible things 'out there', and at the same time been suspicious of our subjectivity, which too often retreats into a private world of feelings By doing this, we equate the real with the visible; the invisible, including God, become incredible. But there is a way through this. Bernard Lonergan, the Canadian Catholic theologian, offers what he calls transcendental precepts. If we *pay attention* to what is, if we can *listen to our questions and try to understand* what happens, if we can constantly check out what is true and *reasonable*, if we can make decisions in keeping with that truth and if we can be prepared to be drawn out of our little self, liberated into noticing the other, by being as faithful as we can to our in-built capacity for *self-transcendence*, then we can wake up to the very truth of our existence.[45]

It is at this point I begin to realise that God is not anyone or thing that my mind can conceive, but that the divine is the very subject of my being, and that with Paul I can say 'it is no longer I who live, but it is Christ who lives in me' (Galatians 2:20) All this is a way of saying that we are to fall in love, living out the faith which is born from God's love for us. We are loved into love, called out of our little selves into the reality and aliveness of our True Self. In this way, we can say that genuine objectivity is the fruit of an authentic subjectivity.

'Who do you say I am? Who am I?' Jesus doesn't want me to be doctrinally correct. He's not wanting a creedal statement or a doctrine. He's wanting me. He is asking me to follow him, to be a

---

44 Jane Hamilton, *A Map of the World*, Doubleday, New York, 1994, 388.
45 Michael Paul Gallagher, 'The Peak of Our Freedom: Bernard Lonergan For Today' in *Spirituality*, Dominican Publications, Dublin, Vol. 15, Sept-Oct., 2009, No. 86.

disciple: to 'learn by going where I have to go'.[46] And I can't answer who Jesus is without taking the next step, without saying who I am. An indigenous woman in Australia has captured this perfectly: 'I am beginning to hear the gospel at the level of my identity'.[47] This is the central fact about faith: the faith that opens me up to the mystery of who I am in God. Descartes, the philosopher, in the 17th century, said: 'I think, therefore I am'. Surely faith is asking us to say, 'I am, therefore I think'.

---

46 Theodore Roethke, 'The Waking', in *Selected Poems*, Faber & Faber, London, 1969, 30.
47 Miriam-Rose Ungenmerr-Baumann, *Dadirri*, Compass Theology Review, no. 1-2, 1988, 9-11.

Chapter Three

Jesus is the parable of God

> *'Tell all the truth but tell it slant-*
> *Success in Circuit lies.'*[48]

These lines from a poem by Emily Dickinson are a very appropriate insight into the transmission of the gospel, and a powerful and pertinent comment on Jesus of Nazareth: who he is, how he saw himself, and the manner in which he so passionately communicated his central vision of the Kingdom or Reign of God. 'Telling all the truth' was crucial to the communication of that singular vision, and 'telling it slant' was the process, not simply instrumental but fundamental, because of the very nature of the gospel. The way of indirection is the necessary way of communicating the gospel, for this gospel is both mystery and hidden.

The mystery of God, and of God's Kingdom, while it demands the rigour of probing, questioning and exploring, appropriate to its claim to truth, is ultimately beyond words and reason. The knowledge of God, and the theological truths we speak, are not ends in themselves: they are evocative, rather than explanatory, and such knowledge will always be heart knowledge, the knowledge born out of love, self-surrender and poverty of spirit. And this knowledge is not simply about communication: it has to do with communion, knowing and being known. God is not the subject's grasp of something 'out there', an object among many objects, but a sharing of who God is: 'not exterior evidence, but the secret call

---

[48] Emily Dickinson, *The Poems of Emily Dickinson*, ed. R.W. Franklin, Harvard University Press, Massachusetts, 2005, 1263.

within us'.[49] Revelation is necessarily provisional, for the One who is revealed is neither a concept nor an idea, and is always pointing beyond both image and language, towards a reality too deep for words.

We should not be surprised then that Jesus chose to speak in parables when he spoke about what he saw was so central in God's relationship and hopes for Israel. And nor should we be surprised that in telling the stories and parables of the coming Kingdom or Reign of God, his own person and identity were at stake, and that he himself was the very parable of God, the very medium of his message.

The New Testament scholar, N. T. Wright,[50] in talking of the centrality of Jesus' message about the Kingdom of God, is clear about the context of that message, where Israel was not simply an 'example' of a nation under God, but was destined to be the very means through which the world would be saved, and that this vocation of Israel, guided by 'love and justice, mercy and truth' would eventually bring renewal and healing to all creation.

What Jesus offers, is not a way of quietism, compromise or zealotry – all possible options to the Jews in Jesus' day – but a Kingdom model, 'equally Jewish if not more so', a way of reading the signs of the times with all their theological and cosmic significance. And this is precisely why his use of parables is so decisive in speaking of a situation where the mysterious reality of God breaks into his hearers' lives, a situation longed for but startling and in so many ways scarcely recognisable.

The parables of Jesus are his commentary on a crisis that faced Israel, but they also serve as a universal challenge precipitating a personal crisis of recognition, acknowledgment, and decision. Jesus was at the very least a prophet of the coming Kingdom, declaring that Israel's long exile was coming to a close: this was not a call to abandon Judaism, but to become 'the true,

---

49 Olivier Clement, quoted in Kallistos Ware, *The Orthodox Way*, NY, St Vladimir's Seminary Press, 1979, 18.
50 N. T. Wright, *The Challenge of Jesus*, SPCK, London, 2000, 18-34.

returned-from-exile people of the one true God'. The parables, focused as they were on the plight and call and future of Israel, clearly challenged his hearers in first century Palestine, to be not only the People of God, but a sign for the whole world. Which allows us – as latter day hearers of the parables –to hear a 'story of invitation and decision'[51] in the face of an imminent irruption of God into our world.

This prophet and teller of parables draws us into our own stories, calling us not so much into interpreting them, but being ourselves interpreted, addressed and challenged – albeit in often confusing and teasing ways. Parabolic language relies for its effectiveness by taking us more deeply into our everyday reality, disrupting the way we so often think and offering us the chance to see our reality and the reality of God, in an entirely new and transformative way.

C. H. Dodd's[52] understanding of the parable remains pertinent: 'At its simplest the parable is a metaphor or simile drawn from nature or common life, arresting the hearer by its vividness or strangeness, and leaving the mind in sufficient doubt about its precise application to tease it into active thought'. The metaphor brings what is familiar into an unfamiliar context, acting disruptively, so as to call attention to it anew, and bringing it into an altogether new frame of reference. As someone has said, the parable is a 'paradigm of reality',[53] but seen in a novel context, based on a 'logic of grace'.[54]

The mistake we sometimes make is that we assume the parable is a means to teach us something, for example, about the graciousness of God, when in fact we are shown an example of ordinary life

---

51 John Shea, *Stories of God: An Unauthorized Biography*, The Thomas More Press, Chicago, 1978, 165.
52 C. H. Dodd, *The Parables of the Kingdom*, Collins Fontana Books, London, 1935, 1961, 16.
53 Robert W. Funk, quoted in Sally McFague, *Speaking in Parables: A Study in Metaphor and Theology*, SCM Press, 1975, 2002, 57.
54 Funk, op. cit., 57.

transformed by grace itself. This suggests that the parable in effect does not *have* a message but *is* the message itself. Hearing a parable of the Kingdom is not so much about gaining a certain knowledge about the Kingdom (though that is a perennial temptation for us), but offering the hearer the possibility of being confronted by the challenge and invitation of the Kingdom itself.

The aim behind the telling of parables for Jesus was not the imparting of correct concepts about the Kingdom but the possibility of a genuine encounter whereby the hearer could make life-changing and life-making choices. The parable has been called a 'linguistic incarnation',[55] a phrase that beautifully brings together the reality that Jesus not only spoke in parables but was himself the parable of God. Grace is the mystery at the heart of every parable, lying hidden beneath stories that are secular, embodied and everyday.

Put simply, *Jesus* told *stories* to *people*. The primary focus, in so many ways, is on the listeners, but the decisive power of those stories rested on *who* and *what* the stories said. By focusing on the stories themselves – and this is the only way forward – we can, like the original hearers, actually hear the authentic voice of the narrator, and the transformative power of his vision. And part of that power is the parable's focus on telling all the truth, but telling it slant, for the way of indirection draws us away from conceptualising belief and allowing us to ground ourselves in the ongoing process of believing and knowing, the lived experience and response to grace that is never an achievement but is always a gift.

Stories, and story-telling belong intrinsically to the human condition. Stories save us from our tendency to be reductionist, for they can – when they reach us – stretch, extend and expand us. They invite us towards a richer and larger life. They help us 'gather all the fragments', and open us towards possibility. They offer us alternative ways of seeing and being; they provoke curiosity, help us make connections, challenge our unacknowledged assumptions,

---

55 McFague, op. cit., 59.

competitiveness and envy, and act, as Kafka saw, as a 'kind of ice-axe to break the frozen sea within us'.[56]

Stories matter – to individuals, families, communities and nations. As Australians, for example, there are always elements of our story we forget or even choose to forget. And it is our loss. We are empowered and enriched by stories of the First Nation peoples, and truth-telling is such an important part of this. But neither can we forget the years of the Depression, the stories of two World Wars, stories of women, migrants and refugees. Stories are important because the heart is reached, not by reason, but by the imagination, and because of their capacity to tap into mystery, into inexhaustible truths, and allow us to journey forward with hope into the unknown.

Jesus told stories, and in particular, parables, which by-pass logic and reason even, stories which leave us dangling, luring us into realms of possibility, shocking us out of our comfortable illusions and deceptions into waking up and seeing, when we so often do not, or cannot, see. They tease us into places beyond even our comprehension, places that question and challenge us into new ways of being, relating and choosing. Just as we cannot pin down the meaning of the parable, it comes as little surprise to realise that we cannot pin down the teller of these parables, nor can we wrap him up in doctrinal statements, that probably say more about our need to control, understand and defend our position.

Jesus was clear about one thing as he told his parables. The Kingdom of God – which is nothing less than the revelation of God – does not come 'with observation', does not come directly, and his question was always: 'how shall we liken the Kingdom of God?' His parables do not illustrate homely truths but point – through everyday stories of wedding feasts, unjust stewards and prodigal sons – towards a profound mystery, often in barely comprehensible ways, which bewilder and discomfort.

---

56 Franz Kafka, in a letter to a childhood friend, January, 1903.

Everything we can say of God is provisional and incomplete, hidden, and is indicated only by ambiguity and irony, by metaphor and simile. Of course the parables tell us a lot about the Kingdom, but even more than that, they offer us the 'means of bringing it to birth'.[57] Walter Bruggemann writes: 'The deep places in our lives – places of resistance and embrace – are not ultimately reached by instruction ... [They] are reached only by stories, by images, metaphors and phrases that line out the world differently, apart from our fear and hurt'.[58]

The realism of the parables shock our imaginations, and offer us an attractive, alternative and imaginative invitation out of destructive patterns of living; and make possible new life. They ask us to live as honestly as we can, even while we cannot see clearly: they even ask us to have the courage to be wrong in order that we might hear a new truth.

So the dispositions we bring to the parable are of crucial importance. We must not be too eager to interpret a parable: it is not spoken to us so that we can grasp its meaning, nor claim a particular insight, but it is offered as an invitation into an encounter with mystery that addresses us, however unsettling that might be. The parable calls for a 'severer listening', a willingness to read and re-read it, to hear it and let it penetrate us. It calls out from us an openness and a patience, where we face and let go of our need to understand, to 'stand under' the parable, and 'to allow it to make its own impact upon us, to receive from it whatever it may "say" to us' at any given time or situation.[59]

As we get in touch with the parables of Jesus, it is vitally important to recover their original meaning. For quite early, the particularly trustworthy tradition that the parables represent, underwent a certain amount of re-interpretation – in a process called the 'hardening' theory – where they began to be treated

---

57 N.T. Wright, quoted in James Martin, SJ., *Jesus: A Pilgrimage*, HarperCollins, NY. 2014, 201.
58 Walter Brueggemann, quoted in Martin., op cit. 201.
59 W. H. Vanstone, *Fare Well in Christ*, DLT, London, 1997, 27.

as allegories, in an often unconscious need to discover a deeper meaning in the simple words of Jesus. For this reason, we now need to look at some verses from Mark's Gospel (4:11b-12), which, by almost universal consent, are among the hardest in the whole gospel to interpret: 'To you has been given the secret of the Kingdom of God, but for those outside, everything comes in parables: in order that "they may indeed look, but not perceive, and may indeed listen, but nor understand; so that they may not turn again and be forgiven"'.

This suggests that Jesus spoke in parables so they could conceal the mystery of the Kingdom of God from those 'outside' and to harden their hearts. Allegorical interpretation, in other words, was the only way to discern that hidden meaning. But what biblical scholarship has made clear is that these words of Mark were 'not a part of the primitive tradition of the words of Jesus but a piece of apostolic teaching', and that they refer, not to the parables but to the whole of Jesus' teaching. So we do not need to look behind the parables for a hidden and secret meaning which can only be grasped through allegory, but simply affirm that Jesus' proclamation of God's rule is bound to remain a riddle, 'in order that no-one will glory in his own knowledge and everyone will live by the miracle of God's grace alone'.[60]

There is little doubt that 'understanding' is, in some ways, an ambivalent term. For the disciples themselves – privileged as they were – can only come to a fuller understanding later, after the crucifixion. The challenge for us today is to recognise the urgency and directness of Jesus' parables, to recover their definite historical setting, and affirm that Jesus spoke to real men and women, in the concrete reality of the moment.

The central thrust of Jesus' message surfaces in the parables, again and again, through constantly changing images. Listening to the parables requires openness, honesty, and a willingness to forgo an interpretation so as to let the parable speak into our life. If we

---

60 Eduard Schwiezer, *The Good News According to Mark*, SPCK, London, 1970, 94. Dodd, op. cit., 15.

are too quick to sum up, lay blame or praise anyone in the story, this may speak of our own blind spots and projections. The day of salvation is here, Jesus declares, in both his parables and in his person, just as the shoots and the leaves herald the summer in the parable of the Fig Tree. The good news is that the new age is here and Jesus has come as Saviour to the poor and to sinners. Now is the time: but can I hear that the parables of the Lost Coin or the Lost Sheep might be addressed to me, by a God who wants the lost to be found and redeemed, and who rejoices at their return home?

In the parable of the Two Sons, the son who says he will go into the vineyard to work, but doesn't, leads to Jesus declaring that 'tax collectors and prostitutes are going into the Kingdom of God before you', for they believed John when he came preaching. For it matters, not so much what we say, but what we do. In the parable of the Two Debtors, Jesus speaks to Simon the Pharisee where Simon's unspoken criticism of Jesus' attitude to the sin-burdened woman is placed within a larger, more generous framework of God's forgiveness. In the parable of the Prodigal Son, or –perhaps more accurately – the parable of the Father's love, Jesus describes in wonderful simplicity the extravagant love, goodness and mercy of God. It is, like so many of the parables, not quite as straightforward as we might first think: initially, we find ourselves on the side of the younger son, ready to overlook his outrageous behaviour to his father, and at the same time unable to see beyond the older son's seemingly hard, unloving and ungenerous actions, who, like so many of Jesus' hearers, find it difficult to abandon their resistance to the gospel. And how should we assess the father's actions, for they would have looked foolish and demeaning in the cultural context of the day?

The parables of the Mustard Seed and the Leaven are parables of contrast, not simply highlighting a natural phenomenon of growth, but celebrating that out of the most insignificant beginnings God creates his mighty Kingdom. The parable of the Seed growing secretly is an encouragement towards faith, that in the present, and indeed in secret, the undisclosed nature of the coming Kingdom is already a reality. And the parable of the Friend who was asked for help at Night speaks of how much more will God hear us when we are in need. And then there is the crisis parable of the Ten Maidens, imploring us not to ignore God's call that all is now ready. In the parable of the Rich Man and Lazarus, Jesus ends with the crushing statement: 'if they do not listen to Moses and the prophets, neither will they be convinced even if someone rises from the dead', emphasising that 'we are saved by hearing', by obedience, and not by a miracle.

And, finally, there is the parable where the Kingdom is like treasure hidden in a field, 'which someone found and hid: then in his joy sells all that he has and buys that field', suggesting that hearing what God is offering is an overwhelming experience of the greatest of all discoveries. Joachim Jeremias suggests that the parables 'compel [Jesus'] hearers to define their attitude towards his person and mission' – the secret and the certainty that 'the hour of fulfilment has come'.[61] In graphic and utterly realistic, everyday terms, the poor and the beggars are summoned to the banquet, lepers are cleansed, the powers of evil have met their match, and the Father's heart is always open.

One of the things that has always struck me, especially as I read in the gospels the many miracles that Jesus performed, is that my insatiable quest to understand them robs them of their mysterious power to 'speak' into my life and situation as it is. This has led me to realise that the real miracle of Jesus of Nazareth is not his walking on water or turning water into wine but the manner in which he was with people. He seemingly created the space for people to be themselves: he elicited from them their deepest hopes and fears; he respected them, listened to them, and offered them stories that had the potential to enlarge their horizons, and to discover, amid all their fears of their own weaknesses and failings, the courage to believe in themselves and discover their God-given giftedness.

Here then, as we think about the parables of Jesus, and the invitation they offer: as we listen patiently and repeatedly to his

---

[61] Joachim Jeremias, *Rediscovering the Parables*, SCM Press, 1966, 181.

words, something shifts in us. However important his words and his stories are – and they are crucial – it is the person of the narrator of these stories, his very identity and personal authority that speaks so fundamentally to us and into our lives. As I have already said: the medium is the message. All this throws light on the church's call to be a witness to this living parable of God, especially in a time when the church does not seem to be speaking into the lives of many of our contemporaries. How can we today live with, interpret and arrange the primary data of the faith in such a way that it can be heard and responded to in life-giving ways? The parables tell us that encounter is more important than insight (for there is always the danger that by gaining a so-called 'insight' we might close off any possibility of a genuine life-changing encounter).

They suggest that the doctrinal truths of the church are secondary and less important than learning to live *our* truth. And they tell us, through story, just how important the imagination is, how it can reach the deepest part of our being, speak the language of transcendence, and move us to action. Re-imagining our world, and the mystery of the Divine at the heart of everything that is, offers us, through the dispositions of patience, waiting and openness that the parables have taught us, the courage to leave behind life-denying choices and find the life which is life indeed.

The story, though it is not technically a parable, that speaks to me so decisively of the challenge of Jesus, the parable of God, is the story of the encounter between so-called 'doubting Thomas' and the Risen Christ (John 20:26-29). Of course, after the shock and the grief attending to the ugly crucifixion of the one he both followed and loved, Thomas was bereft. Of course, he must bring all his dashed hopes and fears to the forefront of his grief. He must bring all his questions and doubts, for if Jesus is ever to be real to him, then he must be real himself. It is now, when Jesus shows him his wounds, his hands and his side, that the parable of God confronts and challenges, confounds and unsettles Thomas. Now is the time for this parable of God, in an encounter both shocking, wounding and liberating, to unveil the hidden truth of Thomas' life. For Jesus' wounds are Thomas' wounds: Jesus' story is Thomas' story: Jesus' death is Thomas' death: and Jesus' life is Thomas' life.

The coming together of the words of Jesus and his identity as God's parable, speaks into Thomas' life, in such a way that he, more deeply than he undoubtedly could ever understand, experiences the coming together of his own life, vocation and identity, so that he can say from the bottom of his heart: 'My Lord and my God!'. The parable of God, whose words not only speak the truth but the very truth of Jesus' own existence, speaks directly and authentically into our lives and the very truth of our existence: his story is *my* story, *our* story: 'it is no longer I who live, but it is Christ who lives in me' (Galatians. 2:20).

C. H. Dodd quotes from one of Jesus' parables: 'I came to bring fire to the earth, and how I wish it were already kindled!' (Luke 12:49). Dodd talks of the 'volcanic energy' of the life of Jesus recorded in the gospels, and says that his parables are no 'leisurely and patient exposition of a system by the founder of a school'.[62] Far more than that, all that Jesus did and said in his life found its fulfilment in his crucifixion and resurrection, which, of course, is the life-giving but confronting parable that continues to live and speak so eloquently into our lives.

---

62 C. H. Dodd, op. cit., 23.

Chapter Four

'We have in us a marvellous mixture of well-being and woe'[63]

> The title to this chapter – Our life is a 'marvellous mixture of both well-being and woe' – is from Julian of Norwich's *Showings (Revelations of Divine Love)*, Chapter 52. Numbers in brackets throughout the text referencing quotations from Julian indicate the chapter from Julian of Norwich, *Showings*, eds. Edmund Colledge, O.S.A. and James Walsh, S.J. Paulist Press, New Jersey, 1978

Thomas Merton was arguably the most celebrated monk and prolific spiritual writer of the twentieth century. And at the heart of his writings was an honesty that helped him see his own inconsistency and absurdity; and lead him to the reality and promise of paradox: 'I have had to accept the fact that my life is almost totally paradoxical. I have also had to learn gradually to get along without apologising for the fact, even to myself .... [it] was and still is a source of insecurity, [but] I have come to find it the greatest security. I have become convinced that the very contradictions in my life are in some ways signs of God's mercy to me; if only because someone so complicated and so prone to confusion and self-defeat could hardly survive for long without special mercy'.[64]

---

[63] First published in *Eremos* August 2022. Reprinted by permission.
[64] Thomas Merton, quoted in Parker Palmer, *The Promise pf Paradox: A Celebration of Contradictions in the Christian Life*, Ave Maria Press, Notre Dame, 1980, 17.

Such insight was both revelatory and transformative, and paradoxically, pure gift. 'My fall into inconsistency was nothing but the revelation of what I am.'[65] 'I am thrown into contradiction: to realise it is mercy, to accept it is love, to help others do the same is compassion.'[66]

Contradictions are statements with elements that are logically at variance with one another, whereas paradox appears to be self-contradictory but on further investigation may prove to be essentially true. If we can refuse to flee from the tensions that life brings us, we can discover the gift and transformative power that paradox carries. Like a parable, or a Zen *koan*, contradictions boggle the mind and give us opportunities either to enter or evade the mystery of God. They do not ask us to abandon our critical faculties or to forgo our questions, or deny the obvious tensions that life and experience bring. We do not claim to clear things up so much as to become a little clearer,

Paradox helps us live with the subtleties of lived experience. Paradox contains both energy and promise, an astonishing secret at the heart of life, a 'shy truth' as Michael Leunig says, that is waiting to be discovered and lived. It was why he could say: 'There are only two feelings. Love and fear'.[67] Leunig said that the universal fact of being human is that we experience a crucifixion and a resurrection every day. In similar vein, Rowan Williams, former Archbishop of Canterbury, said that 'there are two abiding facts: un-reconciled pain and unexhausted compassion'.[68]

Paradox is the natural language when we attempt to talk about God. For the fifteenth century theologian Nicholas of Cusa, God was the supreme paradox, a 'coincidence of opposites':[69] God

---

65 Thomas Merton, *Learning to Love: The Journals of Thomas Merton*, Volume 6, 1966- 1967, Harper, San Francisco, 1997, 106.
66 Thomas Merton, *Learning to Love*, 355.
67 Michael Leunig, *A Common Prayer*, Dove: HarperCollins, Melbourne, 1990.
68 Rowan Williams, *Open to Judgement: Sermons and Addresses*, DLT, London, 1994, 55.
69 Cyprian Smith, *The Way of Paradox*, DLT, London, 1987, 26.

who became human; God who is three, but one; the Saviour who is executed as a common thief; God whose power resides in vulnerability and weakness, whose wisdom is foolishness, and who proclaims a Kingdom that is here yet still to come. Jesus, who proclaimed this Kingdom, is a King who rides a donkey, who says that 'when I am weak then I am strong', and who promises that 'in losing my life I shall find it'.

This is a God who offers me liberation in all the places I least think to look, in brokenness, fear, disappointment, disillusion, limitation and death. To find light we go to the place of darkness, to find fulfilment and wholeness, we go to the place of emptiness and poverty, and to find life, we go to the place of death.

In the fourteenth century, amidst a world where there was much cause for anxiety and despair – a time of heresy and theological confusion and ecclesiastical turmoil, the running sore of the Hundred Years War and the Black Death – Julian of Norwich wrote her *Revelations of Divine Love*. The tensions and contradictions of life that faced her and her fellow Christians became the focus for many years of wrestling and reflection. As an Anchoress who had become gravely ill, she 'conceived a great desire to receive three wounds in my life, that is, the wound of true contrition, the wound of loving compassion and the wound of longing with my will for God' (2). Julian knew that it is our wounds, our vulnerability and incompleteness, where we can confront our falling and our poverty. And it was her wound of compassion that enabled her to experience and understand from within the sufferings of the wounded and crucified God.

Julian's insight helps us in our understanding of what lies at the heart of the Christian revelation, and at the same time, helps us realise how we might appropriate that truth in our very human, everyday experience. Wrestling for years over her lived experience, she realised that, 'During our lifetime here we have in us a marvelous mixture of both well-being and woe' (52). This enabled her to say: 'Peace and love are always in us, living and working, but we are not always in peace and in love' (39). She came to see that the issue was not a question of 'either/or' but always 'both/and'. This tension, which we all face, is never resolved by ignoring or denying either of the poles between which our lives are stretched, but is to be embraced and accepted as the very ground for our growing understanding of the truth.

Julian's attitude to her life experience is precisely what the poet John Keats described as '*Negative Capability*, that is when [one] is capable of being in uncertainties, mysteries, doubts, without any irritable reaching after fact and reason'.[70] The mystery that paradox holds out for us is that we have the chance to touch perfection in imperfection, the sacred in the profane, and hope in despair. Julian's great gift to us was her relentless questioning, and her courage to face the dreadful tension within. With her insights to help us, we can learn to live creatively beyond the surface form of contradiction, and discover the depth and richness at the heart of life, the 'hidden wholeness', the underlying unity of all things. Christian faith proclaims that in Christ the radical distinction between sacred and profane, nature and grace, the infinite and the finite, has been overcome.

It is not surprising that Thomas Merton was drawn to Julian. He prayed to have a 'wise heart' and realised the 'rediscovery of Lady Julian of Norwich will help me'. He was impressed with the fact that she was 'a true theologian with greater clarity, depth, and order than St Teresa (of Avila): she really elaborates, theologically, the content of her revelations. She first experienced, then thought, and the thoughtful deepening of experience worked it back into her life, deeper and deeper, until her whole life as a recluse at Norwich was simply a matter of getting completely saturated in the light she had received all at once, in the "shewings", when she thought she was about to die'.

Here Merton explores Julian's disposition and theological method, how in ever deepening reflection on her experience she was able to come to find a balanced approach towards the contradictions she felt so keenly, and come to some more mature

---

70 D. J. Enright and Ernst de Chikera, eds., *English Critical texts*, OUP, London, 1962, 257.

and transformative acceptance of the richness of paradox. Her 'wise heart' was able to discern what Merton calls *'an* eschatological secret', at work already within all things by which 'all manner of things shall be well'. This secret 'final answer to all the world's anguish' has already been decided, and is a 'great deed', a deed of mercy and of life, already fully at work in the world and 'ordained by Our Lord from the beginning'. And Merton continues: 'This is, for her, the heart of theology: *not solving the contradiction, but remaining in the midst of it,* in peace, knowing that it is fully solved, but that the solution is secret, and will never be guessed until it is revealed' (italics mine).[71] This secret is the key to our life: it is nothing but a revolution in our consciousness, where we realise we are one with him and in him, and in fact, one with all that is. The contradictions remain, but they are no longer the problem.

Julian grasped, and was grasped, by a vision of the crucified Christ that enabled her to see that 'we are one with Christ in his human suffering', and to centre her life on the human image of God and the divine image of humanity. Our eternal identity is assured in the crucified one: the seeming contradiction of the revelation of God crowned with thorns matches the incongruity of Julian's emotional response to it. As she gazes at Christ's bloody head, she tells us 'in the same revelation, suddenly the Trinity filled my heart full of the greatest joy' (4). All of us, at least in our more honest moments, know how easily we can live in illusion, and refuse to face the darkness that lies at the root of the Christian revelation. The crucial point lies in this identification of humanity in the person and sufferings of Christ, 'knowing that God is not destroyed or divided by the intolerable contradictions of human suffering'.[72]

Julian wrestled for a long time over the mystery of sin. For her, sin has no substance, yet 'it is the sharpest scourge with which any chosen soul can be struck' (39). She wondered why, because of the

---

71 Thomas Merton, *Conjectures of a Guilty Bystander*, Doubleday, Image Books, New York, 1968, 211-212.
72 Rowan Williams, *Open to Judgement*, 179.

great wisdom of God, 'the beginning of sin was not prevented' (27). But she knew that sin was inescapably a part of life. 'We need to fall, and we need to see it: for if we did not fall, we should not know how feeble and how wretched we are in ourselves, nor, too, should we know so completely the wonderful love of our Creator' (61). She could see clearly that 'the reason we are oppressed by [our sins] is because of our ignorance of love' (73).

Julian was confident in her reasoning, yet is aware of reason's limitations. She knew that faith was not about reducing mystery to rational certainty, for the heart of human experience is neither consistent nor total chaos, but contradiction. She learned that there was another way of knowing, more akin often to unknowing, offering us a kind of breakthrough where we discover we are known before we know, which only the heart and the imagination, and not the mind, can comprehend.

She could say: 'Some of us believe that God is almighty and may do everything, and that he is all wisdom and can do everything, but that he is all love and wishes to do everything, there we fail' (73). 'For we do not fall in the sight of God, and we do not stand in our own sight; and both of these are true, as I see it, but the contemplating of our Lord God is the higher truth' And she continues: 'But our good Lord always wants us to remain much more in the contemplation of the higher, and not to forsake the knowledge of the lower' (82).

Her complete and intimate focusing of Jesus, in his passionate and compassionate loving, and so graphically imaged in the contradiction of the Cross, allowed her to see how real and close his identification with all of humanity really is. This allowed her to stay with the contradiction, and not try to solve it. It is, above all, her searing honesty and authenticity that opens her up towards the objective truth of God's love. 'We have in us our risen Lord Jesus Christ, and we have in us the wretchedness and the harm of Adam's falling ... And so we remain in this mixture all the days of our life' (52). And yet, in spite of such contradiction and pain, 'he touches us most secretly' and 'protects us so tenderly' (40). This is the God, she realises, who does not stop loving us in our falling, and at the same time does not want us to fall into despair.

Julian sees sin as necessary (27), but for her, the way forward lies in our disposition or attitude towards God. We need balance, and patience, recognising and accusing ourselves of sin, but not wallowing in remorse either. God is not angry, and does not blame us, but looks at us with pity. Sin is simply the way things are, and so God's looking at us 'with pity, and not with blame' is also the way things are. And her tremendous insight into God ran parallel with her insight into the human person. 'For in every soul which will be saved there is a godly will which never assents to sin and never will' (37). Her imaginative insight into the truth of God and humanity allows her to see that 'sin shall not be a shame to mankind, but a glory': healing is possible, when we offer our divided and contradictory self to God who still sees our wounds 'not as wounds but honours' (39).

Julian's 'anchored presence' suggests quite powerfully that in our quest to experience the divine we need to form 'habits of the heart', habits that alert and open us to the mystery of divine grace. Such habits mean that we will live deliberately, intentionally, attentively, intelligently, facing the hard questions, and always willing to seek the truth with openness and a vulnerable heart, knowing that that is what opens the human heart and unlocks the heart of God. Our heart is that mysterious place where we either surrender to God or refuse to do so. Jesus invites us back into our hearts, to hearts of flesh and not stone: and such a heart speaks to us of a more visceral, embodied relationship with mystery.

This is the heart that speaks to us of depth, wisdom, imagination and courage. For the imagination has the power, unlike reason, to bridge the gap between matter and spirit, and to hold multiple dimensions of truth in unity. Its truth is both embodied and experiential, and its language is evocative rather than explanatory. It is the heart that opens us up towards the mystery of our knowledge of God and of ourselves. True knowledge becomes ours when we live as authentically as we can, and are overtaken and grasped by reality in an altogether new way. Such knowledge is akin to falling in love. As Pascal saw, 'The heart has its reasons of which reason knows nothing'.[73]

Just as we know the presence of the soul through its complaints, so it is with the heart; but it is our ignorance of who we really are before God, and not our faults, that hold us back. Made in the image of God, we naturally reflect the relational, mutual community of the Trinity: we become most fully human when we realise our inherent capacity for self-transcendence. Our hearts speak to us of our already God-given gift of both availability and openness. Julian saw and experienced – after much interior struggle and honesty – that unconditional love is our true nature.

Jesus' diagnosis of the human condition is that we can't see, and even when we can, we don't see properly. Jesus says that the pure in heart will see God, but this is not about trying harder or perfecting our virtue. We need to be 'single in heart', to face things as they are, to see the reality which is the source and substance of all creation, and ourselves as manifestations of that reality. For Jesus, the Reign of God is a kind of metaphor, a place we come from rather than a place to go, a state of consciousness and a whole new way of seeing. So repentance, which is the key to the Kingdom, is putting into practice this 'purity of heart', where we begin to realise that we are victims of a mistaken identity.

We must not deny the 'lower' or relative truth of 'not always (being) in peace and love', but at the same time hold firm to the 'higher' or absolute truth that 'peace and love are always in us, living and working'. No wonder Jesus could say that the person who tries to keep their 'life', this smaller life that I think is the whole me, will lose it, and the one who loses that life will find the life which is life indeed.[74]

---

73 Blaise Pascal, *Pensées*, trans. A.J. Krailsheimer, Penguin, Middlesex, 1996, 423.
74 Cynthia Bourgeault, *The Wisdom of Jesus: Transforming Heart and Mind, - A New Perspective on Christ and His Message*, Shambhala, Boston & London, 2008, 10.

Julian 'desired many times to know what was our Lord's meaning in the revelations she received', but it was 'fifteen years after and more, [that] I was answered in spiritual understanding. (86). 'Love is (indeed) our Lord's meaning', which allowed her to experience the reality of God, and realise too that Love is *our* meaning. It has been said that our contradictions are treasures, 'treasure that we have in earthen vessels', creative places, not so much waiting to be resolved but accepted and embraced, as part of the profound and complex movement of growth that constitutes being human. Such contradictions that face us all, carry with them, in all their puzzling and seemingly impenetrable brick walls, opportunities for us to celebrate the transformative, renewing, freeing and hopeful power and promise of paradox.

Chapter Five

'Listen to the language of your wounds'[75] Living in a wounded and wounding world[76]

A few years ago, I read the autobiography of the great Protestant theologian Jurgen Moltmann, titled *A Broad Place*. Moltmann was a POW in Scotland in 1945: he and his fellow prisoners had just been shown photographs of the horrors of the concentration camps, and were dealing with the nightmare realisation that they had been fighting for a regime responsible for unimaginable atrocity. Moltmann had little Christian background and no theological education, but when an army chaplain distributed copies of the Bible, 'I read Mark's Gospel as a whole and came to the story of the passion; when I heard Jesus' death cry, "My God, my God, why have you forsaken me?", I felt growing within me the conviction: this is someone who understands you completely, who is with you in your cry to God and has felt the same forsakenness you are living in now ... I summoned up the courage to live again'.[77]

Almost fifty years ago, when I was in my early twenties and wrestling with issues around faith, God and growing up, I heard, as if for the first time, this same searing cry of abandonment; I heard it as Jesus identifying with us in our worst moments. A little later,

---

75 Jim Cotter, *Waymarks: Cairns for a Journey*, eBook, January 16.
76 First published in *Eremos* August 2020. Reprinted by permission.
77 Jurgen Moltmann, *A Broad Place: An Autobiography*, SCM Press, London, 2007, 30.

sometime in 1972, I – along with the rest of the world – saw that heart-wrenching and intimate photo of a little naked Vietnamese girl, running away in terror from a napalm attack. It was at that moment I instinctively knew that this Jesus was not offering us a particular way of being religious, but a universal way of being human.

No wonder that Moltmann could write these words in *The Crucified God*: 'When the crucified Jesus is called the "image of the invisible God", the meaning is that this is God, and God is like this. God is not greater than he is in this humiliation. God is not more glorious than he is in this self-surrender. God is not more powerful than he is in this helplessness. God is not more divine than he is in this humanity'.[78]

We live in a very wounded and wounding world, a visibly untransformed world, where it is not obvious that God is in charge. And each of us carries wounds, wounds of the past, memories of betrayals and jealousies, theft and abuse. These wounds are deeply personal, relational, societal and global. And to find some meaning and hope we must 'gather all the fragments' of our lives, however painful, negative, or shameful they might be. For 'the goal of Christian life is not enlightenment but wholeness – an acceptance of this complicated and muddled bundle of experiences as a possible theatre for God's creative work'. We must be ready 'to be questioned, judged, stripped naked and left speechless by that which lies at the centre of [our] faith'.[79]

It is as if Jesus is saying to us: 'I come to wound you and to heal the wound'.[80] The Cross wounds us too, allowing us to see this crucified man's story: his personal inner experience of extreme suffering and abandonment is actually the breakthrough allowing

---

78 Jurgen Moltmann, *The Crucified God*, SCM Press, London, 1974.
79 Rowan Williams, *The Wound of Knowledge*, DLT, London, 1979.
80 Kevin Hart, 'The Companion', *New and Selected Poems*, Angus & Robertson, Sydney, 1995, 87.

us to experience, as he did, even in our worst moments, a God who is a power 'cherishing people and making them free'.[81]

Perhaps we need to say that Jesus died not so much for our sins, but because of them: that at the heart of our faith is this bitter place of rejection and betrayal. We are victims, and we are the maker of victims. But Jesus comes to us as the 'forgiving victim',[82] offering us a freedom that tells us that we are in the right place when we are poor, not knowing and powerless. Far from passively accepting what is, we discover our inherent capacity to meet the pain and anguish of life through acceptance and hope, and in this struggle grow into a new human-ness, 'more capable both of pain and love'.

This new 'human-ness' is not a possession, but a new life, opening up for us new possibilities. It is not an assured accomplishment, but rather a learned day-by-day way of being and living with what is so often absurd, bitter, contradictory. We stand defence-less and unprotected, our only security in this weak, vulnerable, impotent man on a cross. In the poet Rupert Brooke's memorable words, forged in the nightmare of World War One: 'Safe though all safety's lost'.[83]

There is a long tradition in Scripture and the Christian story that suggests it is in our wounds, our wounded-ness, and even in our woundings that we can find healing. In fact, the Christian tradition has it that God is the one who wounds us in order to heal us. In the book of Job, it is said: 'For he wounds, but he binds up;/ He strikes, but his hands heal' (Job 5:18). St John of the Cross cries out: 'You have wounded me in order to cure me, O divine hand'.[84] The English television commentator, Dennis Potter, in his last interview before he died, said: 'Religion is always the wound,

---

81 Edward Schillebeeckx, *Jesus*, Collins, London, 1974, 1983.
82 James Alison, *Knowing Jesus*, SPCK, London, 1993, 37.
83 Rupert Brooke, *The Poetical Works of Rupert Brooke*, ed. Geoffrey Keynes, Faber & Faber Ltd., London, 1946, 20.
84 St. John of the Cross, 'The Living Flame of Love', in *The Collected Works of St. John of the Cross*, transl. by Kieran Kavanaugh. O.C.D. and Otilio Rodriguez. O.C.D., Institute of Carmelite Studies, Washington DC, 1979, 601.

never the bandage'.[85] Through our wounds, God finds a way into us that is not possible when we are invulnerable, safe and secure. Our wounds can become doorways into discovering the goodness of God. They are not waiting simply to be fixed: they are the very path towards wholeness.

In *Sabbatical Journey*, Henri Nouwen wrote:

> 'What to do with this inner wound that is so easily touched and starts bleeding again? It is such a familiar wound. It has been with me for many years. I don't think this wound – this immense need for affection, and this immense fear of rejection – will ever go away. It is there to stay, but maybe for a good reason. Perhaps it is a gateway to my salvation, a door to glory, and a passage to freedom'.[86]

And what of this comment from Nicholas Wolterstorff, in *Lament for a Son*, writing about the trauma and wounding of his small son's death?

> 'I shall try and keep the wound from healing, in recognition of our living still in the old order of things. I shall try to keep it from healing, in solidarity with those who sit beside us on humanity's mourning bench'.[87]

Both Nouwen and Wolterstorff testify to the given-ness as well as the giftedness of our woundings. The wound of self-knowledge for Nouwen becomes a gateway into freedom: Wolterstorff's wound of grief becomes, extraordinarily, an invitation into solidarity with all who mourn. Our wounds can become the first stirrings of faith, alerting us to our inherent capacity for compassion, and opening us towards living with a measure of hope.

The starting points for faith are very human places, they are 'limit' or 'boundary' experiences of everyday relationships, failure,

---

85 Dennis Potter, last Interview, New York Times, 12 June 1994.
86 Henri Nouwen, *Sabbatical Journey: The Diary of his Final year*, DLT, London, 1998, 25.
87 Nicholas Wolterstorrf quoted in David Ford, *The Shape of Living*, Fount Paperbacks, London, 1997, 154.

pain, or loss. Faith is a practised way of living, It is a gift, not a possession, an attitude, not an opinion. It tries to make sense out of what we experience here and now. It is not a life of answers and foregone conclusions, but an invitation into liminal and dark places where, as Richard Rohr says, we can't fix, or understand or control.

Faith sees the difference between surface and depth, between what is transient and what lasts. It grows in the face of reality, will admit to doubt, and always seeks to be both honest and courageous. It is a hard-won realisation that despite the things that go wrong, despite the tragedies that mar and disfigure so much of the creation, life can be lived with compassion and hope. Life can be trusted. Faith extends and challenges us to the very core of our being. It means letting go and dying to the smaller vision of life and of ourselves that is simply inadequate for the journey. Faith helps us see a more distant horizon, waking us up to hitherto unseen depths, opening us up to hidden riches and seeds of new life that are always wanting to germinate.

Julian of Norwich wanted to experience more deeply the love of the Crucified. She prayed for three wounds: the wound of contrition, the wound of compassion, and the wound of true longing.[88] Her wound of contrition is the beginning of faith – that openness to reality, to things as they are, that refuses to live in an illusory peace, however awkward reality might be. The wound of compassion is the entrance into love, which alone makes sense of the brokenness of the cross. Compassion asks us to enter into places of hurt and confusion, and challenges us to cry out with those in misery, mourn with those who grieve, and weep with those in tears. It is nothing less than full immersion into what it is to be human.

The truth that God reveals about God-self is that God is fundamentally oriented towards the other, that God is a self-emptying, self-communicating, self-giving love for the sake of the other. 'Love is ...a journey, an ongoing exodus out of the closed,

---

[88] Julian of Norwich, *Showings*, eds. Edmund Colledge. O.S.A. & James Walsh S.J., Paulist, New Jersey, 1978, Chapter 2.

inward-looking self towards its liberation through self-giving, and thus towards authentic self-discovery and indeed the discovery of God'.[89] And it is this truth of God that Jesus came to show is our truth too: we flourish when we give ourselves away. This spirituality of the Exodus calls us into a school of love, the workshop of the new humanity, where we confront this life-and-death struggle between the self and the other and wake up to and accept our inherent capacity for self-transcendence. Our only hope is to fall in love with love. But there is a cost. Herbert McCabe, a Dominican and lecturer in theology and philosophy in Oxford, liked to say: 'If you do not love, you will not be alive: if you do love effectively, you will be killed'.[90]

So as we live compassionately and in faith, we bring our total situation into a wider context, offering a larger horizon and greater depth, and we discover both a measure of hope and meaning that makes sense of our lives. The third wound Julian asked for was the wound of longing and desire: this is the wound of hope, that bears witness to that which is in us 'that will not acknowledge conclusion', that will not rest until all the facts are in.

Hope is not optimism – 'not the conviction that things will turn out well, but the certainty that something makes sense, regardless of how it turns out'.[91] Hope is both gift and task: it is grounded in reality, rooted in memory, and oriented towards the future. It cannot grow or thrive in evasion or denial. It is about being willing to stay where we are and to live to the full in the belief that there is something hidden here that will reveal itself. Hope is a state of mind, a dimension of the soul, and an orientation of the heart. It isn't about waiting for things to get better 'out there'. It is about getting better 'in here', about getting better about what is going on in us.

---

89 Benedict XVI, *Deus Caritas Est*, St. Paul's Publications, Sydney, 2006, 13.
90 Herbert McCabe, *God Matters*, Continuum, London, 1997, 218.
91 Vaclav Havel, *Disturbing the Peace*, Vintage Books, New York, 1991, 181-2. and *Letters to Olga*, Faber & Faber, London, 1988.

Some of the great witnesses to hope in the seventy or so years since the Second World War are the extraordinary testimonies of those who have discovered hope while in prison. Brian Keenan, the Beirut hostage, said of that time, that captivity had help us realise 'an extraordinary capacity to unchain ourselves from what we had known and been – and to set free those trapped people and parts of ourselves'.[92]

Solzhenitsyn, lying in a Gulag prison on rotting straw, could exclaim: 'Bless you, prison!'[93] Dietrich Bonhoeffer found in prison a freedom of spirit, a gift where somehow he felt the closeness of God. Nelson Mandela was free, well before he was ever released from prison, free to forgive and become an agent for reconciliation. And Desmond Tutu , fighting against the evils of Apartheid in Southern Africa, used to famously say, that while he wished God would make it more obvious that God was in charge – [but] 'we do not lose hope – because we are prisoners of hope'.[94]

One of our problems is that we find it hard to believe in God because we do not have a lively imaginative picture of the relationship between God and the world. Far from dismissing the imagination as imaginary or fantasy, we need to see that the imagination is really the only way we have of handling the world. It is the meeting place between God and human beings. It evokes, rather than explains. It gives insight, and releases energy. Made in God's image, we are image-bearers and image -makers. The imagination speaks the language of transcendence. Through what is familiar, we bump up against the unfamiliar. It gives form to things unseen.

If we do not befriend the imagination, we are vulnerable to despair. We need a particular disposition of patience to see beyond present realities. Instead of being hijacked by the present crisis or trial, or 'reducing' our lives to negative thought, we need to nurture our imagination, activate our memories and remember patterns or moments of grace which have touched us in the past.

---

92 Brian Keenan, *An Evil Cradling*, Vintage, London, 1992.
93 Alexander Solzhenitsyn, *The Gulag Archipelago*, transl. Thomas P. Whitney, Collins Fontana, 1974.
94 Desmond Tutu, in an interview with *Christianity Today*, October 5, 1992.

The imagination tells us nothing new but revives our awareness of what we already know, and deepens that awareness.

But the question remains: is the imagination enough? Is thinking differently or seeing things differently enough? Hope – in a quote widely attributed to St Augustine – has two daughters: anger at the way things are, and courage that propels a person so that things do not stay as they are. In the Kingdom or Reign of God Jesus offers us an attractive, imaginative alternative to the way things are, as well as the capacity to be and to work for the change that we wish to see in the world. In this sense, we could say that 'Images are forms of transport. They get us going: they move us on'.[95]

The world is not as it should be. The church is not as it should be. And as we get in touch with things as they are – the ecological crisis, the irreconcilable Israeli-Palestinian conflict, the coronavirus pandemic, church disunity, abuse or domestic violence – hope asks us to get in touch with the 'dangerous memory' of Jesus and the Cross. Hope dares us to connect with something that is radically beyond human control: God's self-disclosure in history, a God who is helpless and weak, but a God who is with us in the solidarity of love. Such a 'dangerous memory' – which is what faith is – loosens the grip of dominant claims about the way life is, and it releases in us longing for a different way.

The Cross and Resurrection say to us that what we are experiencing now is not the final word but a call to resistance, protest and lament. Here, in the stark place of the prison cell, the prison we all experience in one way or another, where hopes and dreams are broken: it is here, in weakness and failure, in our wounds and woundings, where the one thing which cannot be taken away is the freedom to choose. It depends on God. It depends on us! Hope is not abdication, for God cannot be fully God unless we are fully human and fully alive. In this wounded and wounding world, 'Love [remains] the goal, but faith is the process of getting there, and hope is the willingness to live without resolution or closure'.[96]

---

95 Anselm Gruen, *Images of Jesus*, Continuum, London, 1992, 4.
96 Richard Rohr, *Things Hidden: Scripture as Spirituality*, St. Anthony Messenger

Chapter Six

Prayer

'God's breath in man returning to his birth' [97]

When writing about prayer, a good place to start is where Monica Furlong began her book *Contemplating Now*, citing the words of Lao Tzu in the *Tao Te Ching*: 'One who knows does not speak; one who speaks does not know'. As she saw so clearly: 'The dangers of talking pretentious rubbish in this field are great: the chance of having wise and useful things to say is slight'.[98] For there is a kind of absurdity in putting into words the unspeakable, yet the very need to talk or write speaks not of what one has fully experienced or achieved, but of what one longs for. And it is that desire or longing which strikes at the very character of prayer.

The many ways of prayer

There are, of course, many ways of prayer: spoken or vocal prayer, personal or private prayer, as well as corporate and liturgical prayer, the prayer of intercession, silent prayer, the prayer of reflection and meditation, and the deep prayer of contemplation. And who hasn't, at some stage of their life, prayed? Of course, the issue of

---

Press, Cincinnati, 2008, 55.
97 George Herbert, 'Prayer (1)', *The English Poems of George Herbert*, ed., C. A. Patrides, J.M. Dent & Sons Ltd., London, 70.
98 Monica Furlong, *Contemplating Now*, Hodder and Stoughton, London, 1971, 5.

God is – for many people – problematical: but that hasn't stopped many of us from crying out for help in difficult or painful or fearful circumstances. That very cry from the heart – however real and painful it might be – is, in so much of our common human experience, a cry of anguish that too often seems to go unheard.

This 'silence' from a God 'out there' only intensifies our bewilderment in thinking about God, and for many of us – even though we find ourselves in extreme circumstances, again and again crying out to be heard by *someone* – this experience means that we become more and more distant from any sense of a divine reality that is actually there for us and for our good. But then there are those of us who persevere, still in the land of unknowing, but who sense that, in the harsh realities of life, there must be 'something more', and, when we are as real as we possibly can be, find there the possibility of meeting a God who is real.

Those of us, who for one reason or another, have sensed in the person of Jesus a common humanity, have been strangely attracted by his inner life of prayer, a life in many ways transparent and open to us in the pages of the Gospels. His is an inner life that appears grounded, real and embodied, appreciative of the goodness and wonder of creation, and at the same time open to the griefs, fears, harshness and even terrors of a very real human life. So we have persisted: we have possibly read of others in their journey of prayer; we have tried various forms of prayer; we have tried sitting still, and being silent; we have sometimes given up, and started again; and while there have even been moments of 'success', there have been many moments of failure.

When we try to think about our prayer, we notice how obsessed we can be about getting answers, remaining self-centred, and miss, it seems, the relationship that is on offer. We feel confounded by our experience of absence and 'unknowing', and often fail to see that this deeply felt experience could be a turning point in our journey of prayer. For this is a genuine crisis, where we face, as if for the first time, our very real inability to pray, a crisis which could prove to be the indispensable next step in this, now recognised, longed-for journey that we are making.

'Surely the Lord is in this place....'

André Louf says the 'the first and most fundamental truth about prayer is to know that we are unable to pray. "Lord, teach us how to pray"'.[99] Many of us do the best we can, but it seemingly isn't enough. We reach a stale-mate, a dead-end, and at this point in our journey we need to hear Thomas Merton: 'It is a risky thing to pray, and the danger is that our very prayers get between God and us. The great thing in prayer is not to pray, but to go directly to God. If saying our prayers is an obstacle to prayer, cut it out!.... the best way to pray is; Stop! Let prayer pray within you'.[100]

For the point of prayer is not that it is prayer that we seek, but God. So our inability to pray, our impotence, our 'unknowing', turns out to be the place for us to be. It is, in fact, our place, the right place where, in our poverty, we can learn to stay, and find, as St Paul found, that it is 'in weakness that the power of God is made perfect (2 Corinthians 12:10). It is as if God is taking prayer out of our hands, for only then will we be able to let go of our need to accomplish or try harder, but simply surrender to God's activity in us. Like Jacob, it is here, in this place, where we can begin to wake up and say: 'Surely the Lord is in this place – and I did not know it' (Genesis 28:16). Prayer is still open to us, but it seems on God's terms!

And the place of prayer? It seems we are to listen in the place where it is already happening. For the tradition is very clear. A Byzantine monk found it hard to explain where or how this happened for him: But 'Looking back, my impression is that for many, many years I was carrying prayer within my heart, but did not know it at the time. It was like a spring, but one covered by a stone. Then at a certain moment Jesus took the stone away'.[101] The crisis – of realising that we are unable to pray – becomes an

---

99 André Louf, *Teach Us To Pray*, DLT, London,1974, 11-12.
100 Merton quoted in M. Basil Pennington, *Centering Prayer: Renewing an Ancient Christian Prayer Form*, Image Books, Doubleday & Inc., NY, 19
101 Louf, op. cit., 22.

awakening, a breakthrough to an awareness, a coming to birth. Thomas Merton, in a talk not long before he died, put it boldly: 'In prayer we discover what we already have. You start where you are, you deepen what you already have, and you realise that you are already there. We already have everything, but we don't know it and we don't experience it. Everything has been given to us in Christ. All we need is to experience what we already possess'.[102]

It all 'boils down to giving ourselves in prayer a chance to realise that we have what we seek'. Prayer is nothing less than a restoration, a finding of our real treasure, our real or True Self, a celebration of the Kingdom or Reign of God that is within. Augustine was clear: 'Man (sic) must first be restored to himself that, making in himself as it were a stepping-stone, he may rise thence and be borne up to God'.[103]

The inner experience of Jesus

The one thing we do know from the gospel accounts of the disciples is that, despite their weakness, their not seeing, hearing or understanding what Jesus was doing and saying to them – not dissimilar to us – was that they were attracted when they saw Jesus praying: 'Lord, teach us to pray' (Luke 11:1). It is clear that Jesus experienced a deep one-ness with the divine source. On his first step to his public ministry, he could say that 'the Spirit of the Lord is upon me' (Luke 4:18). In his humanity, this meant a deep surrender of the human ego to the divine Self: he learned to listen, to be obedient. The agony in the Garden and on the cross were times of intense suffering, which point to an act of self-displacement or self-emptying (*kenosis*), where divinity relinquishes all claims against humanity and where a vulnerable

---

102 Merton quoted in James Finley, *Merton's Palace of Nowhere*, Ave Maria Press, Notre Dame, Indiana,1978, 111.
103 Augustine quoted in John Main, *The Inner Christ*, DLT, London, 1987, 16.

Jesus fully accepts the consequences of being present in a violent world, declaring that human failure is not the end but a beginning.

Yet Jesus' inner journey is also one of intense spiritual bliss. Here is someone who lived and spoke out of a transformative and constant awareness that God – Abba Father – was both with him and within him. We are also discovering in our age, that Jesus' Father-related language – a culturally inherited understanding and experience, and what we might call the fundamental I-Thou relationship – grew out of a Mother-related experience of the divine. Here the Mother is the primal 'I', indicating not an inter-personal relationship, which Jesus spoke of, but an intra-personal relationship.[104]

All of which reaches towards, and unfolds into a trans-personal one-ness with the divine, signalling complete surrender and transformation in the divine. We are not isolated individuals but, reflecting the God 'in whom we live and move and have our being', persons-in-relation, discovering that self-transcendence is the essence of existence, and that 'self-actualisation is possible only as a side effect of self-transcendence' for 'Being human always points, and is directed, to something other than oneself....'.[105]

Sebastian Painadath[106] suggests that when Jesus said in John's Gospel, 'I am the stem, you are the branches', he was suggesting that we are to make the same inner journey that he made. *Just as* the Father sent me, so do I send you into the world'(John 17:18). *'Just as* the Father knows me, I know my own'(John 10:15). *Just as* the Father loved me, so will you remain in my love' (John 15:9, 17:26). *'Just as* I draw life from the Father, so will you draw life from me'(John 6:57). *'Just as* I am in the Father, and the Father is in me, so am I in you and you are in me' (John17:21, 14:20). And

---

104 Sebastian Painadath, S.J., *The Spiritual Journey*, ISPCK, Delhi, 2007, 20-23. I am indebted to Fr Sebastian for his insights into the two primordial symbols of father and mother in speaking of the Divine.
105 Victor Frankl, *Man's Search For Meaning*, Beacon Press, Boston, 1959, 133.
106 Painadath, op. cit., 58.

'*Just as* the Father and I are one, so you may all be one in us' (John 17:21-22).

The Greek preposition *kathos* (just as) is hugely significant, for Jesus wants us to make the same inner journey, and participate in the same inner experience that shaped his consciousness. Which suggests that we are to find deep freedom from a superficial ego-centred self-identity in a deeper, God-centred 'life according to the Spirit'. Just as Jesus, animated by the Spirit, lived and breathed the inner-trinitarian life of the divine, so we too are to live and breathe that same trinitarian life. When Jesus says that he is the bread of life, the living water, the light, the way, and the truth these are not simply objectifying symbols out there, but assimilative symbols that speak so clearly that we are in him and that he is in us. When we pray, it is not us, but Jesus who prays in us, embodying and expressing the very life of the trinitarian community-of-love. Jesus is the true subject of my being: with Paul we can say that 'It is no longer I who live, but it is Christ who lives in me' (Galatians 2:20).

'Blessed are the pure in heart'

Now, of course, our life is not always consciously experienced at this level. The gospel repeatedly has Jesus saying that the disciples' hearts are blind and closed, slow to listen, weighed down with pleasures and sorrows. Such self-centredness, stubbornness, and hardness of heart, are part of our common humanity, but are at the same time the raw material that can be transformed into a heart of flesh (Ezekiel 36:26). The 'eyes of the heart' need to be enlightened (Ephesians 1:18) by the power which is the Holy Spirit 'which opens eyes that are closed, hearts that are unaware and minds that shrink from too much reality....(for) vision and vulnerability go together'.[107] In the Beatitudes, Jesus says: 'Blessed are the pure in heart, for they will see God' (Matthew 5:8). Such 'purity of heart'

---

107 John V. Taylor, *The Go-Between God*, SCM Press, London, 1972, 19.

is genuine wisdom. It has nothing to do with being virtuous or moral, so much as singleness of mind, where our heart is a unified whole.

William Blake put it boldly: 'If the doors of perception were cleansed, everything would appear to man as it is, infinite'.[108] The journey into prayer is a 'return to the heart, finding one's deepest centre, awakening the profound depths of our being in the presence of God who is the source of our being and our life'.[109] And this is nothing less than a journey into the wonder of our own creation. And this way to the heart is far from looking for a 'method' or a 'system' of prayer: it has to do with attitude, outlook, and disposition. It is being both attentive and intentional, where we wake up to the extraordinary reality that our heart is already in a state of prayer: for this is the birthright of every human being, made as we are, in the image of God. We carry this hidden treasure always within us: as Jesus said: 'The Kingdom of God is among you' (Luke 17:21).

Of course, this is a never ending process, but a gradual becoming conscious of what we have already received. So what ever resources we might use, there is only one objective: finding our heart, letting go of the dross and the pre-occupations and anxieties of the mind which so easily dominate us, and even convince us that this is really who we are, and discovering the hidden and true self, the 'I am' at the centre of my life.

The heart is an imaginative metaphor for the centre of the human being. It is the source of all physical, emotional, intellectual energies: it is the seat of the will and our moral compass. From the heart arise hidden impulses as well as conscious feelings and thoughts, moods and wishes. It is the centre of perception and understanding. It is the fount of compassion, the central and unifying organ of our personal life. The mind is obviously useful and important: but is not to be the place we live out from. But

---

108 William Blake, quoted in John Main, *The Inner Christ*, DLT, London, 1987, 28.
109 Merton quoted in Finley, op cit., 99.

neither is the heart a sentimental refuge. As Pascal saw so clearly: 'The heart has its reasons which reason does not know about'.[110]

The heart speaks to us of our longings and restlessness, which Augustine spoke of: but 'I can only look for something that I have, to some degree, already found. How can I search for beauty and truth unless that beauty and truth are already known to me in the depth of my heart?'[111] So here is the very place where we encounter God: for 'He is on the inside of our longings'.[112] Prayer is both 'a consciousness of one's union with God' and at the same time 'an awareness of one's inner self'. The miracle of prayer is the realisation that each of us is 'a member of a race in which God himself became incarnate', despite, as Merton saw so clearly, all 'the sorrows and stupidities of the human condition'.[113] He knew that we carry within us the divine reality: 'a point of nothingness which is untouched by sin and by illusion, a point of pure faith and 'this point of nothingness and of absolute poverty is the pure glory of God in us'.[114]

Merton loved Julian of Norwich who could say: 'For in every soul which will be saved, there is a godly will which never assents to sin, and never will'. It is out of this 'marvellous mixture of well-being and woe'[115] that we can begin to let the stream of living water and prayer pray within us. So the tradition is clear: in the words of the Russian mystic Theophan the Recluse: 'To pray is to

---

110 Blaise Pascal, *Pensées*, Penguin Books, 1966, 110.
111 Henri J. M. Nouwen, quoted in Margaret Magdalen, CSMV, *Furnace of the Heart: Rekindling Our Longing For God*, DLT, London, 1998
112 Maria Boulding, *The Coming of God*, Fount Paperbacks, London, 1984, 8.
113 Merton quoted in Robert Faricy, S. J., *Praying*, Villa Books, Dublin, 1979, 61.
114 Thomas Merton, *Conjectures of a Guilty Bystander*, Doubleday and Company, 1966, 157-158.
115 Julian of Norwich, *Showings*, eds. Edmund Colledge, O.S.A. & James Walsh, S. J., Paulist press, NY, 1978, chaps. 37, 52.

descend with the mind in the heart, and there to stand before the face of the Lord, ever-present, all-seeing, within you'.[116]

'What I do is live. How I pray, is breathe'[117]

Prayer – according to the poet-priest George Herbert – is 'God's breath in man returning to his birth'. The simplest place to start is what constitutes the very 'heart' of being human: and that is to acknowledge and pay attention to our breathing. We find a comfortable position, and after a few moments of noticing our surroundings, any noises, or bodily aches or pains, we settle down, and begin to get in touch with our breathing in, and breathing out. We take time over this, noticing the passage of air through our mouth or nostrils, and filling our lungs with air as we breathe in, and exhaling, emptying our lungs of air.

This breathing is something we share with every human being on the planet. And then we remember the Genesis story: where the first human being was made out of the dust of the earth, and God breathed into him and made him a living being. As part of humanity, and part of the whole created order, God breathes in us and through us, grounding us in the earth, connecting us with every human being, and opening us up to the very life and Spirit of God. Here I begin to experience a new inner freedom. I am utterly dependent as a creature of 'borrowed breath' (Wisdom 15:16), yet at the same time I begin to experience a primordial 'yes' that is not my own, nor at my disposal: it is simply a 'given', a wonderful, yet mysterious 'yes' of being itself.

Our breathing is a kind of mirror to our psyche: as we are, so we breathe. When I am worried or anxious, my breathing becomes shallow. As I sit still, attentive to my breathing, I become aware of a constant stream of feelings and thoughts: I notice them, and

---

116 Theophan the Recluse, quoted in Henri Nouwen, *The Way of the Heart*, DLT, London, 1982, 76.
117 Thomas Merton, quoted in Finley, op. cit., 107-8.

acknowledge them, and, staying focused on my breath, let them go, one by one. In this way, over time, I experience a movement within that goes below the surface of my mind, towards my heart, my inner self: discovering that the aim is not mastery, which is beyond me, but an acknowledgment of mystery: the mystery of life, and its preciousness.

And as I explore my heart, there is much that is beyond thought and understanding: but there is a sense that this too is like treasure, hidden within me, a treasure that is simply waiting to be lived. We are not builders, but diggers, entering more deeply into the mystery of our being. And through attention I begin to get a sense of our creator God within, reaching out towards me in this present moment, addressing me from within, addressing me in such a way that I begin to find myself.

As we enter into our deeper and true self, we can begin to accept the way things are in our world. What has caused us anguish or anger, resentment or pain, we can begin to see things simply as they are, in touch with what is. Of course, there are some things that we can do, or change and make a difference: and we need to do so if that is at all possible. But there is much that simply is, and instead of wrestling, arguing and pleading that things should be different, which so preoccupies our minds, leading us to think this is the real me, we can approach what is within our hearts, and find the treasure that we have always been, but too often missed: and this is not an escape route, but the fertile ground for compassion and the recognition of the 'other' as pure gift.

Here I begin to discover something about myself that I have struggled with in the past: my insecurities, ignorance and unknowing, my competitive nature and my low self-esteem. Here, addressed in the silence I find myself, as known and loved, accepted and free. 'Love is the reason for my existence ... Love is my true identity ... Love is my name'.[118] I AM is calling me to be who I am, and to begin to live out of this deep inner truth. And here I realise

---

118 Merton, *New Seeds of Contemplation*, New Directions Paperback, NY, 1962, 1972, 60.

I can and want to be open, as open as possible, so as to receive what good things God wants to give me. It was Augustine who said that God is always wanting to give us good things, but our hands are too full and busy and preoccupied to receive them.

Prayer then is nothing less than waking up to the fact that there is so much more to me than the superficial and pre-occupied self that has dominated my everyday life. That 'self' is only a small part of who I really am, and as I begin to acknowledge this, I realise, with Simone Weil, that 'Waiting patiently in expectation is the foundation of the spiritual life'.[119] This is the journey we are called to: to pray, or better put, to let the Spirit pray in us: to wake up and begin to see clearly, with 'purity of heart', for 'Our whole business in this life is to restore to health the eye of the heart whereby God may be seen'.[120] And in 'poverty of spirit' to recognise our vulnerability, weakness and unknowing, and our inability to pray, and in self-emptying and self-surrender, to be both open and receptive and blessed, which is the only possible way to receive the good things God wants always to give us.

---

119 Simone Weil, *First and Last Notebooks*, OUP, London, 1970, 99.
120 Augustine, quoted in John Main, op. cit., 40.

Chapter Seven

The Prayer of Asking

'What we most truly want is what we most really are'

> The quotations from Julian of Norwich are from her *Revelations of Divine Love*, trans. Clifton Wolters, Penguin Books, London, 1966, 1973, and are referenced by 'Julian' followed by chapter number.

Petitionary prayer (asking God for things), or the prayer of intercession (praying for others), raises fundamental questions around the relationship between God and humanity, between God's will and human wills, where 'eternity and time meet in the contingency of human desire'.[121] When we ask something in prayer, we are immediately confronted with this intersection between the divine and human wills, the immanent and the transcendent, the finite and the infinite, the contingent and the absolute. Such an intersection – as we become more and more aware of it – is both our most amazing gift and most difficult problem. It offers us the theological task of exploring the nature of God and the nature of the human being, and how they belong together. This meeting point between divinity and humanity is the central issue that faces us, and rather than evading it or hiding behind facile answers, the way forward is accepting this as a given

---

[121] Turner, Denys, *Julian of Norwich, Theologian*, Yale University Press, North Haven, 2011, 166. The title of this chapter is also from Turner, p. 204.

in our lives, which, if responded to openly and freely, can become a place of grace, discovery and transformation.

Prayer as asking

The 'problem' of intercessory prayer is that it is a paradox between God's foreknowledge and our free-will, and as a paradox remains an 'amazing mystery', not a problem to be solved but a mystery to be explored and lived. The more we 'attempt to test the efficacy of prayer experimentally suggests that [we consider] prayer is impersonal and manipulative',[122] but learning to follow Jesus leads us to affirm the fundamental assumption that our relationship with the mystery of God is both personal, intimate and responsive. For when we pray we find ourselves addressed, created as partners in a dialogue.[123] So we cannot 'solve' the problem as if it were a problem 'out there', because we are already a part of it.

Whenever we pray we are already caught up with the answer. So intercession is not about finding the right technique, or treating it like a business transaction or a contract: the language of prayer is the language of communion, a communion between friends, and assumes a covenantal, and not a contractual, relationship. As Jesus said to his disciples, 'I call you friends' (John 15:14-5). And rather than establishing this fundamental relationship, the prayer of asking is both a recognition of, and a response to, the communion that already exists between God and us. God spoke to Julian of Norwich in the fourteenth century: 'I am the foundation of your praying. In the first place my will is that you should pray, and then I make it your will too, and since it is I who make you pray, and you do so pray, how can you not have what you ask for?' (Julian 41)

---

122 Brunner, Vincent, *What Are We Doing When We Pray? A Philosophical Inquiry*, SCM. London, 1984, 7.
123 von Balthasar, Hans Urs, *Prayer*, SPCK, London, 1957, 1973, 19.

We cannot read the Gospels without realising that Jesus himself enjoyed a deep intimate communion with God, whom he called Father. Everything he said and did flowed out of this inner experience, grounded and tested and challenged in prayer. While it is clear that he understood that prayer involved both thanksgiving and confession, his teaching about prayer focused almost exclusively on the prayer of asking, surely his affirmation of the conjunction between God's providence and our dependence. 'Ask, and it shall be given you' (Matthew 7:7; Luke 11:9). 'Whatever you ask in prayer, believing, you shall receive' (Mark 11:24). 'Whatever you ask the Father in my name, he will give it to you' (John 16:23).

In response to the disciples asking 'Lord, teach us to pray', Jesus gave them what we now call the Lord's Prayer, which is fundamentally a prayer of petition, framed within a vision of the nature of God and the promise of the Reign of God. And it is a vision that Jesus knew would be the catalyst for us to discover in ourselves both the confidence and trust in the providence, goodness and will of God.

Iris Murdoch, the English novelist and philosopher, goes so far as to say that 'prayer is properly not petition, but simply an attention to God which is a form of love. With it goes the idea of grace, of a supernatural assistance to our human endeavour which overcomes empirical limitations of personality'.[124] Such attention suggests that intercession is a form of prayer that is contemplative. As we gather all our concerns, anxieties and hopes, we are drawn – through such attention, care and patience – into an ongoing process, a new space, where, in the continual exercise of our freedom, we become more and more attuned to the gracious, expansive and generous vision that God has for the whole of creation. Our confidence and hope are based, not on information so much as on the character of God revealed to us in the Christ-event..

---

124 Murdoch, Iris, *The Sovereignty of Good*, Routledge & Kegan Paul, London, 1970, 2001, 53-4.

Science and theology

Intercession is a constant part of the Christian biblical, liturgical tradition; and for those who seek to follow in the way of Jesus there is no doubt concerning its centrality. Yet for many Christians, there are real questions about such prayer: questions concerning God's omniscience, providence, and omnipotence; questions about God's freedom and our freedom, and the place and usefulness of the prayers of asking; questions about God in the context of a world shaped by natural causes, many of which are well explained by science. Yet despite the extraordinary advances that science has made, science cannot tell us everything: there remain questions of meaning around our lives and our deaths; questions about the restlessness and searching of the human heart and mind which are such a significant feature of human lives; and questions around love and forgiveness, and the meaning of the universe, all of which are more theological and philosophical questions rather than scientific ones.

Christian theology sees God as the Creator, intimately present to every part of the universe, and in every way enabling it to be and become. Such a theology takes science seriously, and respects its endeavours. Science is committed to explaining – as fully as it can – the emergence of the universe and the evolution of life, while theology wants to proclaim a God who works creatively and providentially through the whole network of created, or secondary, causes. The action of God, theology asserts, reflects God's goodness and love, and respects creaturely autonomy, dignity and freedom, so that creatures have their own integrity and relative independence as causal agents. The sciences reveal that in the evolution of the universe, there is a direction towards greater complexity. Chance plays an integral part in all of this, all within a process of natural law, providing opportunities of new systems and species. Death, as we share in the evolutionary community of life, is the price paid for living in this complex world, a world where both competition for resources and cooperation continually shape life as it unfolds on this planet.

Our prayers of intercession take place in, and in fact are a part of a mysterious interaction of life-giving and life-enhancing energies, which, when we are one with God in love and will, can move and influence our world and others in ways we can scarcely guess. We certainly do not or cannot pray necessarily with knowledge of the answers yet the very questions that arise within us draw us more deeply into the pain of caring and compassion. Michael Ramsey, former Archbishop of Canterbury, put it succinctly and plainly: 'To be with God with others on the heart, that is intercession'.[125] Real prayer is presence, bringing us closer to God as well as to our fellow human beings. It acknowledges God's compassion which flows endlessly towards all that God has created, and all that God sustains, yet – and this is the mystery – God seems to wait upon the willingness and co-operation of human wills.[126]

Intercessory prayer is grounded in the real

If we want God to be real, we must be as real as we can be, facing our illusions and projections, and expressing our feelings of despair or disappointment, sadness or joy, hope and desire. The reality we face, despite the terrific progress made through scientific discoveries, medical research and human ingenuity, is that suffering on a personal and interpersonal, social and global scale, stubbornly remains a part of the human condition. Our sight and understanding are at best partial and distorted, and we are limited, incomplete and unknowing. And being real means facing the crucial questions that surround our prayers of asking.

Does God in fact hear our prayers? Is it possible that God can be influenced by our prayers? What if God hears our prayers and does not respond? Jesus prayed in Gethsemane in deep anguish

---

125 Ramsey, Michael, *The Christian Priest Today*, SPCK, London, 16.
126 Edwards, Denis, *How God Acts: Creation, Redemption and Special Divine Action*, ATF Ltd., Hindmarsh, 2010. I am particularly indebted to the late Denis Edwards for this book, and this paragraph particularly reflects his thoughts.

and distress. On the cross, he expressed the incomparable pain and torment of forsakenness 'to the edge of despair ...[yet he] did not go over this edge' and nevertheless maintained, as he did all throughout his life and ministry, his intimate conversation with God. The question often asked, after the anguish of Auschwitz, whether prayer is still possible, receives at least a provisional response from the example of Jesus in Gethsemane.[127]

'All the great experiences of life – freedom, encounter, love, death – are worked out in the silent turbulence of an impoverished spirit'.[128] Being real exposes us to a real God. Despite the seemingly endless frustrations, emptiness and utter dependence that we often experience, we are in the right place when we are poor in spirit, and just as it did for Jesus, this can become the place where we find the courage to hope in the face of seemingly hopeless facts and to stay the course. Such an apprenticeship to reality is vital in our becoming more fully ourselves. Even at our most extreme moments, which we cannot evade, we begin to discover that our asking is part of a deeply mysterious exchange, not trying to change God's mind – though we may begin there – but to be changed ourselves, changed in such a way that we are able to receive what God wants to give us. The slow transforming work of grace in the human heart, albeit in the face of unheard or unanswered prayer, disposes us towards our growing in confidence and trust.

As we surrender ourselves, we become, through what we say, not only more aware of who God is but who we ourselves are. However crushing unanswered prayer may be, it can become the means for me to realise that I do not know, and puts me into a position both of dependence and willingness to learn. In our prayers of asking, we are not trying to get God to do something we think needs to be done, but opening ourselves up to what God is doing, in our world, in others and in ourselves, so that we may respond appropriately. The realisation that intercession is a deepening awareness of God, and of others, rather than a request

---

127 Cullmann, Oscar, *Prayer in the New Testament*, SCM, London, 1995, 126.
128 Metz, Johannes B., *Poverty of Spirit*, Paulist Press, New York, 1968, 49.

can become a celebration of our freedom. 'We are not engaged in creating or producing anything, but in becoming aware of what already is the fact, that God is immediate and intimately present both to ourselves and to the one for whom we are praying'.[129]

The beauty and the mystery and the complexity of the prayer of petition is the marvellous discourse between one centre of freedom and another. The very act of asking God points to our underlying relationship with God, and our acknowledgment that God's endless gift to us is that we are able to participate in his will and co-operate with him in its fruit. Properly understood, it means that we discover our capacity for growth and liberation as human becomings. Rather than spending our time hoping for God to intervene, our prayers of asking are surely inviting us to dig more deeply into the human condition and realise that prayer works within the existing potential that is at the heart of creation and within us all. We are incomplete, and there is always more, and while much in our lives is imperfectly understood, our asking is always hinting at the hidden resources yearning for fulfillment that lie within us.

But there is a cost, and the cost is our learning to surrender, in freedom, our will. And that means that our most needed disposition is the capacity to wait: and Julian knew the cost of such waiting. 'Sometimes it seems to us that we have been praying a long time, and yet we do not see any answer. We should not get despondent because of this. I believe our Lord intends by this either that we should await a more suitable time, or more grace, or a better gift' (Julian 42). And in the waiting we discover, that far from being isolated, autonomous beings, we are fundamentally relational, and that we have an innate capacity for self-transcendence and compassion.

The 'other' – far from being a rival or someone to fear – becomes a gift that helps me towards my becoming more fully myself. And as I pray for the 'other', be it a person or persons or

---

129 Baker, John Austin, *The Foolishness of God*, DLT, London 1970.

events, the prayer asks me what action I can do to express that compassion. For 'real prayer leads to action', a kind of exchange, where we experience something of the other's burden. Our actions are, of course, limited and fragmentary, but no less real or effective for that, and the 'reality principle' of such prayer will also save us from the fantasy of 'imagining that we can do for people what we manifestly can't do, and from the anxiety and guilt feelings such fantasies evoke. And praying for people makes us sensitive to their deepest needs which are generally not their most obvious ones'.[130] Our prayer and our actions can then be seen within the vision of our God who is intimately present to all things, and works endlessly and creatively through us.

Our future has already appeared

One particularly helpful way of thinking about God's relationship with the whole created order is to see it in the light of the decisive act of God in the person of Jesus Christ. This immediately places our thinking about intercessory prayer within the context of a Trinitarian, relational God, who expresses God-self in and through the person of Christ, in both his life and in his death and resurrection, and in the sending of the Holy Spirit. The Holy Spirit proceeds from God, and, from within the whole of creation, strives in and with all creatures in bringing them to the Father. The Spirit speaks of the nearness of God, the God who is both without and within, wanting and enabling our response.

This theological insight helps us to see and hear the teaching and healing ministry of Jesus of Nazareth within the context of what Jesus called the Kingdom or Reign of God. As Eduard Schillebeeckx has said: '[Jesus] saw a distant vision of final, perfect and universal salvation – the kingdom of God – in and through his own fragmentary actions, which were historical and thus

---

130 Williams, H.A., *Becoming What I Am: A discussion of the methods and results of Christian prayer*, DLT, London, 1977, 75.

limited and finite'.[131] Such limitations on the ministry of Jesus are an enormous help in our prayers and actions for the good or well-being of others, enabling us to see our intent and actions as participation in and anticipation of God's coming reign, as well as conveying to us the validity of such prayers, however fragmentary and limited they might be.

God's reign will not come about simply as the result of our actions, nor will it come without our being a part of it. St Augustine's pithy aphorism puts it well: 'God without us will not; and we without God cannot'.[132] God always delights in and respects human freedom and the integrity of the natural world, and achieves the divine purposes in and through created causes. God chooses to fulfil the divine intent through actions which always invite our participation and co-operation.

Our faith rests on the conviction that everything has already been accomplished in Christ: yet the paradox is that we live in between times, and the end time is 'not yet'. The dilemma that intercessory prayer brings is the reality that Julian of Norwich wrestled with and came to see as crucial: 'that the greatest deeds are already done' and 'if we pray, not realising that he is already at work, it makes us despondent and sceptical ... and if we see him at work yet do not pray, we do less than we ought' (Julian 42).

Our prayers of petition, far from focusing on their results or effectiveness, engender hope as they are based on the character of God, and focus on what God has done, and is doing. Our prayers, far from trying to change or influence God's designs, become instruments – conceived from all eternity – to carry them out. The real basis of intercessory prayer – seen within the horizon of eternity – rests on a vision of humanity that includes not only those who have been before us but those who will follow, what traditionally is called the communion of saints. With John Taylor,

---

131 Schillebeeckx, Eduard, *Christ: The Christian Experience in the Modern World*, London, SCM, 1980, 791.
132 Borg, Marcus, *Jesus: Uncovering the Life, teaching, Relevance of a Religious Revolutionary*, Harper, San Francisco, 2006, 260.

we can surely say: 'They pray for us ... with clearer understanding, but I for them in ignorance, though still with love. And love, not knowledge, is the substance of prayer'.[133]

These wellsprings of love, imaged for us in the Reign of God as a present reality and a future hope, will come about, not because of God's overriding omnipotence, but through our co-operation and will. It is this unity with God, and the sincerity of our asking for God's grace, that we are able to recognise and admit to our poverty and, far from passively abandoning our own desires, actually desire the accomplishment of God's will. God's kingdom is a reality only through the power of God's love. And that takes effect in human history only through the wills of human beings in whom that love has become the fundamental reality. Julian of Norwich would say 'Love is our Lord's meaning' (Julian 86), and radically and equally true is that Love is our meaning. To begin to pray is to open ourselves to that love, and let it begin to deal with our self-defensive-ness and way-ward and hard hearts, our self-will and desire for all that is negative and life-denying.

Precarious love

Creation is a precarious, vulnerable and patient activity. Because of the incarnation, we can say that God is with us and for us, and is endlessly engaged in seeking and finding new ways to restore and redeem. W. H. Vanstone writes: 'If God is love, and if the universe is His creation, then for the being of the universe God is totally expended in precarious endeavour, of which the issue, as triumph or as tragedy, has passed from his hands ... God waits upon the response of his creation'.[134] God, as it were, stands in the middle of our world and universe and history and invites us to stand where God stands: like God, committed and involved. God is the beloved

---

133 Taylor, John V., *The Go-Between God: The Holy Spirit and the Christian Mission*, SCM, London, 1972, 233-4.
134 Vanstone, *Love's Endeavour, Love's Expense*, DLT, London, 1977

Go-between, the opener of eyes, the giver of life, the One who is there for us. *Preces* is the Latin for prayer, so our prayer for others is always going to be a 'precarious endeavour ', where we learn the real power of intercessory prayer: the power that 'comes to its full strength in weakness', a weakness that 'is stronger than [our] strength' (2 Corinthians 12:9).

The crucified Jesus, the image of the divine participation in the brokenness and suffering of the whole of creation, is at the heart of all true intercession: Christ's passion is nothing other than compassion. Christ prays in us, and in our prayer we are lifted into his act of reconciliation. The choices that face humanity which we are discovering have profoundly influenced and modified evolutionary history, now suggest just how crucial our responsibilities for the universe's and our well-being really are, and indicate that we are co-creators with God. In this understanding, God is intimately involved in the continuing evolution of the whole of creation, holding it in being at every instant; allowing us to see ourselves as organically related to the whole cosmos.

With freedom, self-awareness, and the realisation that we live in a moral landscape, we begin to realise that we can no longer hide behind the endless, unresolvable questions that arise from this intersection between God's will and our will, none of which satisfy our hearts or minds or consciences. Intercessory prayer is nothing less than living responsively, responsibly, and in keeping with our capacity for self-transcendence, and moving beyond ourselves, for the sake of others and the whole creation.

There is undoubtedly the problem and the mystery of suffering, but the choice is not between a God who doesn't act or care, or a God who acts often, and infringes our freedom, or a God, who is arbitrary or manipulative. The occasional stories of miraculous cures and healings don't seem to help much in the context and scale of immense and continual human suffering in our world. John Polkinghorne has written that 'the world's suffering is not gratuitous but a necessary contribution to some greater good which could only be realised in this mysterious way'. God, it seems, 'allows the whole universe to be itself' in a freedom that allows each part of the universe to act according to its nature. In this way, we affirm that 'God is not the puppet master of either men (sic) or matter'.[135]

For Julian, God's goodness and love are the impulse and energy not only of our prayer but are what drives the whole of creation's movement towards fulfillment. Her priority is the prayer itself, not its effectiveness in terms of tangible results. For 'it is not our praying that is the cause of God's goodness to us ... Our lord is greatly cheered by our prayer. He looks for it and he wants it' (Julian 41). Everything else becomes unimportant in comparison to drawing close to God in intimacy and love.

Wherever our prayers begin, they become compassionate responses, not only to our needs, but to the needs of our fellow men and women and of creation, and draw us into the very heart and purpose of God. Our prayers of petition move us into a larger space, marked by gratitude, and where, whatever problems we had about the efficacy of such prayer pale into insignificance. Julian is clear: ask, start where you are, and be as real as possible, and enter into that transfiguring space where you begin to ask for what makes sense of it all: mercy and grace, forgiveness and faith, hope and love. 'Through our ignorance and inexperience in the ways of love we spend so much time on petition. I saw it was more worthy of God and more pleasing to him that through his goodness we should pray with full confidence, and by his grace cling to him with real understanding and unshakeable love ... For in his goodness is included all one can want, without exception' (Julian 6).

Intercession as an apprenticeship in desire

John Burnaby, writing an essay in the book *Soundings* in the early 1960s, wrote: 'if I am to learn what God wants, the way to do

---

[135] Polkinghorne, John, *Science and Christian Belief, Theological reflections of a bottom-up thinker*, SPCK, London, 1994, 83.

it is not to disown the inmost desires of my heart, but rather deliberately to spread them out before God, to face with all the honesty I can achieve the real truth about my desires, to wrestle with the sham of professing desires which are not really my own'.[136] Beginning to see how central to the human condition our wants and desires are is the first step towards realising what we are really thirsting for. It is as if God is drawing us towards himself, but in this life, never fully satisfies us. in Julian's words, 'I saw him and sought him; I had him and wanted him' (Julian 10).

In the seventeenth century, Thomas Traherne, an English priest and poet, was clear that human need was essential to human happiness. 'Wants are the ligatures which tie us to God, whereby we live in him and feel his enjoyments'. Jesus, far from imparting to us any kind of secret knowledge, both challenges our conventional view of God, and extends our understanding of what it means to be a human being, and wants us to see how our knowledge of God and of ourselves are intimately and inextricably bound together. Traherne offers us an insight into the fact that God also wants: wants our happiness and wants us to enjoy God's joys and treasures. He continues: 'This is very strange that God should want, for in him is the fullness of blessedness'. But the dilemma is resolved: God is always wanting and always satisfied. 'God is from all eternity full of want, or else he could not be full of Treasure ... Want is the fountain of all His fullness'.[137]

God's whole being and activity can be expressed in wanting: it is the very law of love, experienced in the mutuality of freedom, where God recognises our freedom so that we can ask things of him rather than forcing them out of him. And we acknowledge God's freedom in the same way – the God who always deals with us with respect and integrity. The manner in which Jesus was with others, which reached its fulfillment in his movement from

---

136 Burnaby, John, 'Christian Prayer', *Soundings: Essays Concerning Christian Understanding*, Cambridge University Press, London, 1962, 234-5.
137 Traherne, Thomas, *Centuries*, Mowbray, London, 1960, First Century, sections 51, 52.

action to passion, seen in the cross, was nothing less than *kenotic*, self-emptying compassionate love. Jesus made visible both the love and the otherness of God, an otherness which is the only guarantee of our freedom to grow to our true spiritual stature.

The love of God is the energy at work to draw us into a true relation with God, which in its turn becomes the pattern of human life. Jesus, we might say, is God's prayer both to the world and for the world, which offers us the extraordinary insight that our prayer, if it is to be prayer at all, is in fact Christ's prayer.

So our prayer then becomes an imaginative and attractive insight into God's loving purposes and dream, for us all and for the whole of creation. Because of Christ, we can say we are loved in the beloved, as the writer to the letter to the Ephesians says. Rowan Williams develops this: 'The whole story of creation, incarnation, and our incorporation into Christ's body tells us that God desires us, *as if we were God*, as if we were that unconditional response to God's giving that [God] makes in the life of the Trinity. We are created so that we may be caught up in this, so that we may grow into the wholehearted love of God by learning that God loves us as God loves God'.[138]

In our prayer, we are putting the riches of our love and compassion at the disposal of God, knowing that our intercession is caught up into Christ's intercession. Far from telling God what God should be doing, our prayer is nothing less than a lifetime's growing, in confidence and trust, into an ever deeper and more intimate communion with God. Such prayer is an apprenticeship, the very schooling of our desires, and becomes 'the place where we sort out our desires and where we ourselves are sorted out by the desires we choose to follow'.[139] In Jesus, we see God's 'Yes' to the whole of creation, and at the same time we see humanity's and creation's 'Yes' to God. In the prayer of intercession, we join our

---

[138] Williams, Rowan, *The Body's Grace: The Tenth Michael Harding memorial Address*, London, Lesbian and Gay Christian Movement, 1989, 3.

[139] Ulanov, Ann & Barry, *Primary Speech: A Psychology of Prayer*, Westminster John Know Press, Louisville, 1982, 20.

'Yes' to that of Jesus, 'the human image of God and the divine image of humanity',[140] where we become most fully ourselves and share with him the 'precarious love' reconciling all things to God.

---

140 Gatta, Julia, *A Pastoral Art: Spiritual Guidance in the English Mystics*, DLT, London, 1987, 75.

www.ingramcontent.com/pod-product-compliance
Lightning Source LLC
Chambersburg PA
CBHW012007090526
44590CB00026B/3908